SEEKING
PEACE IN
AFRICA

Published in association with
Bethany Theological Seminary
Richmond, Indiana

SEEKING PEACE IN AFRICA

Stories from African Peacemakers

Edited by
Donald E. Miller, Scott Holland, Dean Johnson, and Lon Fendall

Foreword by Edward P. Antonio
WCC Foreword by Samuel Kobia

Cascadia

Publishing House
Telford, Pennsylvania

copublished with

World
Council of
Churches
Publications
Geneva, Switzerland

and
Herald Press
Scottdale, Pennsylvania

Cascadia Publishing House orders, information, reprint permissions:
contact@CascadiaPublishingHouse.com
1-215-723-9125
126 Klingerman Road, Telford PA 18969
www.CascadiaPublishingHouse.com

Seeking Peace in Africa
Copyright © 2007 by Cascadia Publishing House,
Telford, PA 18969
All rights reserved.
Copublished with Herald Press, Scottdale, PA and

 World
Council of
Churches
Publications

Geneva, Switzerland;
World Council of Churches ISBN 978-2-8254-1508-5
Cascadia ISBN 13: 978-1-931038-38-6; ISBN 10: 1-931038-38-4
Library of Congress Catalog Number: 2006027647
Printed in the United States of America
Book design by Cascadia Publishing House
Cover design by Anne H. Berry

The paper used in this publication is recycled and meets the
minimum requirements of American National Standard for Information Sciences—Permanence of Paper for Printed Library Materials, ANSI Z39.48-1984.

Library of Congress Cataloguing-in-Publication Data
Seeking peace in Africa : stories from African peacemakers / edited by Donald E. Miller ... [et al.] ; foreword by Edward P. Antonio ; WCC foreword by Samuel Kobia.
    p. cm.
Includes index.
ISBN-13: 978-1-931038-38-6 (pbk. : alk. paper)
ISBN-10: 1-931038-38-4 (pbk. : alk. paper)
1. Peace--Religious aspects--Historic peace churches--Congresses. 2. Violence--Religious aspects--Christianity--Congresses. 3. Violence--Africa--Congresses. 4. Historic peace churches--Doctrines--Congresses. I. Miller, Donald Eugene. II. Title.

BT736.4.S44 2007
261.8'73096--dc22

2006027647

15 14 13 12 11 10 09 08 07   10 9 8 7 6 5 4 3 2 1

*Dedicated to those who gathered at
Watu Wa Amani, Nairobi, Kenya, August 8-14, 2004.*

Contents

PART III: THE STORIES OF VIOLENCE IN ITS MANY FORMS

Stories and personal narratives about the violence, genocide, warfare, rape, AIDS/HIV, corruption, poverty, and oppression that continue to take place in Africa

PART IV: STORIES OF CHRISTIAN PEACEMAKING

Stories that emphasize what the Historic Peace Churches have done internally in response to violence.

PART V: STORIES OF PEACEMAKING IN THE PUBLIC SQUARE

Stories of how the Historic Peace Churches have responded to violence in the public arena

PART VI: THE COURAGE TO HOPE

Stories and meditations about hope amid violence

Foreword

TO MANY PEOPLE THE STORY IS WELL-KNOWN. Africa is indeed a place of darkness, a continent riddled with numerous forms of violence: interminable ethnic bloodletting, HIV/AIDS, and other death-dealing diseases not to mention poverty, hunger, and malnutrition; civil wars; refugees or displaced peoples; and genocide. Given all this, one can be excused for wondering whether anything good can come out of Africa. It is easy to be overwhelmed by the constant barrage of bad news about the continent.

Amid such a potentially discouraging profile, however, *Seeking Peace in Africa* emerges as a refreshing and hope-inspiring collection of essays that attest to the efforts of ordinary Christians to tell a different story, a story about the possibility of a different Africa—one which is not a place of darkness but of hope, grace, and peace. The book is not primarily about theory, politics, philosophy, or theology but about testimonies, stories, anecdotes, tales, and parables of community-based peacemaking up and down the continent.

Yet in framing it within the context of narrative, the editors of these essays have offered us a collection that speaks to Africa's situation at all levels of theory and experience. Here the ordinary person and the theologian or philosopher are given important resources for thinking concretely about peace and violence in Africa. As far as I know, there really is nothing like this book on the market. It is a first. I have no doubt that it will go a long way in helping church and society reimagine African's future.

While taking seriously the continued existence of conflict and violence all over the continent, each and every contributor to the volume refuses to succumb to the Afro-pessimism which has become the hallmark of so much public and official commentary on the future of

Africa. The realism of the narratives is balanced by stories of redemption. It is impossible to overemphasize the importance of these contributions—for they deal with matters of life and death at both the micro-level of individual experience and at the macro-level of the whole continent.

In both cases, the contributions make clear that there can be no viable future for Africa without the essential elements of reconciliation and forgiveness, justice, and peace as well as healing and hope. In addition to being about hope and the future, this is also a book very much concerned with the present. There is no escapism here. On every page we are confronted by the realities of violence and despair.

One of the distinctive features of the book is that although the editors are Westerners, the majority of the contributors are themselves African. This means that the volume embodies a substantial African voice on matters that are fundamentally African. Strange as it may seem, this is a rare achievement, for Africa is a continent whose voice has been historically suppressed or ignored.

A second distinctive element of the book is that it represents a critical Christian intervention in talk about peace on the continent. Among many other things, this is important because of the massive presence of the Christian church in Africa. Too often the discourse on peace and other public matters has been left to politicians and international organizations like the United Nations, even as the church seems to have nothing to say. This book brings the Christian contribution on peace into the public arena and reminds us that peace should be the concern of all and not just politicians.

I fully commend this book to anyone who seriously wants to learn and understand Christian grassroots peace efforts in Africa.

—*Edward P. Antonio*
  Associate Professor of Theology and Social Theory and
  Diversity Officer, Iliff School of Theology
  Denver, Colorado

WCC FOREWORD

THE DECADE TO OVERCOME VIOLENCE (DOV)—Churches Seeking Reconciliation and Peace, 2001-2010, was adopted by the World Council of Churches at its 1998 Harare Assembly. It builds on the previous Program to Overcome Violence, which had begun in 1994 when apartheid had left South Africa with a legacy of violence. The most recent initiative runs parallel to the United Nations Decade for a Culture of Peace and Nonviolence for the Children of the World. It calls churches, organizations, movements, and individuals actively to pursue nonviolence and reconciliation in all their activities.

While the Decade to Overcome Violence is a call to all churches and their members to address the universal problem of violence, the WCC explicitly challenged the Historic Peace Churches (HPC) to share their experiences and insights with the ecumenical movement and to help initiate an ongoing dialogue. Encounters between the HPC and mainline churches on the issues of war and peace happened in Europe after World War II and into the 1960s, but not systematically on an international basis since then and especially not outside Europe and North America.

Fortunately, the HPC network heard and responded to the WCC's call for special attention to the evils of violence. Of course, HPC efforts go back for centuries, but these Christians have since the 1970s been constructive leaders in ecumenical peace efforts. The HPC Continuation Committee in North America, the Friends World Committee for Consultation, the Church of the Brethren, and the Mennonite Central Committee (MCC), all had some experience in peacemaking. Christians in those organizations took the lead in planning and convening a theological consultation in 2001 at Bienenberg Seminary near Basel, Switzerland. This consultation came to be known as

Bienenberg I (and many of its proceedings were published in *Seeking Cultures of Peace: A Peace Church Conversation*, ed. Fernando Enns, Scott Holland, and Ann K. Riggs; Cascadia Publishing House, 2004). On that occasion it became clear that conversation about peace theology and practice could appropriately be done only if it took into account the perspectives of people in the rest of the world, especially in Africa, Latin America, and Asia. It was later decided to schedule this conference in Africa. This direction is wholeheartedly supported by the WCC, whose special focus on Africa is an ecumenical accompaniment to the African churches' search for a new vision for the continent.

The WCC therefore is very pleased to be part of a second theological consultation by the Historic Peace Churches. For the voices of Africans associated with the Historic Peace Churches to be articulated and heard within the ecumenical context, it is important to create platforms, such as this one, for encounter, process, and deliberation. While on some continents the HPC churches are only a small minority of Christians and of the broader populations, in Africa their numbers are substantial. Their history, theology, and witness is invaluable to the church of the twenty-first century. We are confident that the current efforts underway have the potential to engender fruitful dialogue and to empower the voices of the HPC beyond Europe and North America for the benefit of the ecumenical family as it engages in a decade-long journey of overcoming violence.

—*Samuel Kobia (Kenya)*
  General Secretary of the World Council of Churches

EDITOR'S PREFACE

THE ARTICLES IN THIS BOOK ARE TAKEN FROM presentations at the WATU WA AMANI conference that was held in Nairobi, Kenya, August 8-13, 2004 (and some of the presentations were briefly cited earlier in the article by Russell Haitch and Donald Miller, "Storytelling as a Means of Peacemaking: A Case Study of Christian Education in Africa," that appeared in *Religious Education* 101/3, Summer 2006, pp. 390-40, published by the Religious Education Association). The name of the conference is a phrase in the Swahili language of East Africa meaning "people of peace." The purpose of the gathering was to provide an occasion for peace church representatives from Africa along with several peace church leaders from other continents to address the theological, institutional, and praxis issues related to overcoming violence and building peace that arise in the African context.

The conference was held in response to an invitation from the World Council of Churches (WCC) to the Historic Peace Churches (HPC) to share their experiences and insights with the ecumenical church as a part of the Decade to Overcome Violence. The Historic Peace Churches is a designation that refers to the Friends (Quakers), Mennonites, and Church of the Brethren, who throughout their histories have understood peacemaking and resisting violence to be an essential mark of the church. While considering the direction and shape of the Decade to Overcome Violence, the Central Committee of the WCC observed, "We recognize the steady witness of monastic traditions and the Historic Peace Churches, and we want to receive anew their contribution through the Decade" (Minutes of the Fiftieth Meeting, Geneva, Switzerland, 26 August-September 3, 1999, 188).

Responding to the WCC's invitation, representatives from the Historic Peace Churches met in 2001 at the Mennonite Bible School and Seminary in Bienenberg, Switzerland, near Basel. The results of those discussions have been published as *Seeking Cultures of Peace: A Peace Church Conversation* (Cascadia Publishing House, Herald Press, and WCC, 2004). Participants recommended that a second conference be held, but that it take into account the perspectives of people in Africa, Latin America, and Asia. When the planning committee discovered that each of the three HPC communions has more members in Africa than in North America and Europe, it was agreed to hold "Bienenberg II" in Africa. So it was that the three African churches held a conference together for the first time.

Kenya commended itself as a location for the conference because it is a country where the majority of African Friends are located, although Friends are also in Burundi, the Democratic Republic of Congo, Rwanda, Tanzania, and Uganda. Most Church of the Brethren members are located in northern Nigeria, even though Brethren have also been active in Sudan. Mennonites are found in Congo, Zimbabwe, Tanzania, Ethiopia, Zambia, Burkina Faso, Somalia, and Kenya. Because the word *Bienenberg* has no significance in Africa, the Swahili phrase *Watu Wa Amani* was chosen as the name for the conference. The phrase indicates that the focus of the conference was to be a discussion among Africans about what it means for the church to be a "people of peace." Of more than ninety conference participants, most of the speakers and three-fourths of those who attended were African.

Planning for the conference was done by a committee of nine persons, three from each of the Historic Peace Churches. They were in constant touch with the peace churches in Africa as the planning took place. Co-moderators for the event were Agnes Abuom, Kenyan and one of the eight presidents of the World Council of Churches, and North American Donald Miller, convenor of the planning committee and former member of the Central Committee of the World Council of Churches.

The conference was built around telling stories of violence, conflict, and reconciliation that participants brought from their home communities across Africa. The stories were guided by three themes on successive days: Threats to Peace, Christian Faithfulness and the Common Good, and Forgiveness and Renewal. Threats to peace included not only open warfare but also injustice, disease, and poverty. The idea of the common good lifted up radically different religious commitments and tribal loyalties that prevail in many parts of Africa. Forgiveness and renewal opened questions of the role of faith and of the churches in meeting the situations of violence, encouraging reconciliation, and promoting healing. A theological panel provided questions for small group discussion each day. The conference was immersed in worship by having daily morning meditations and devotional services each evening led by the different religious traditions present at the conference. Translation into both English and French was provided for all sessions.

The book is divided into six parts. Part I, entitled "Marketplaces Where Africans Think and Talk About the Common Good," picks up from Samuel Kobia, General Secretary of the World Council of Churches and a citizen of Kenya, the concept that the marketplace (*sokoni*) is a symbol of the free and open exchange of ideas in Africa. Furthermore Kobia argues that such free exchange is needed for Africans to create a new identity and thereby gain the political will to shape their own destiny. Only in this way can Africans address the problems of violence, poverty, and disease prevalent in their continent. Agnes Abuom supports this vision when she calls for open spaces for discussion and the celebration of diversity. The Watu Wa Amani conference and the articles of this book promote a free exchange of ideas in the marketplace, which can lead to a new African identity built on the reconciliation of differences and a continuous effort to formulate the common good. Using Agnes Abuom's metaphor, such open discussion can be the central supporting pole that holds up the house.

Part II is entitled "Heritage of Peacemaking." Paulus Widjaja gives his foundational theology of peacemaking based on his experience working with the tensions between Muslims and Christians in southast Asia. Malesi Kinaro, a Quaker from Kenya; Komuesa Kalunga, a Mennonite from Congo; and Filibus Gwama, a Brethren from Nigeria, discuss the tradition of peacemaking that was brought to them by the missionary founders of their churches in the eighteenth and nineteenth centuries.

Part III addresses "Stories of Violence in Its Many Forms." Ahmed Haile speaks of the way in which Africa is linked to the world-wide networks of political conflict, terrorism and counter-terrorism, something that poses a very heavy challenge to the peace churches. There follow descriptions of violence in Zimbabwe, Congo, Nigeria, Burundi, Rwanda, Ethiopia, and Sudan. While not dwelling unnecessarily on the disturbing details, the stories give overwhelming images of the millions of lives that have been lost and of the untold cost in human suffering.

In view of the stories from Part III, Part IV, "Stories of Christian Peacemakers," is equally compelling in detailing the efforts of the peace churches, often in seemingly insurmountable circumstances. David Niyonzima makes a case for the absolute importance of forgiveness if there is to be any real resolution of decades of violence. Philippe Nakuwundi describes the training programs that have been established in Burundi. Cecile Nyiramana of Rwanda explains the impossibility of getting beyond the horror of genocide there unless people have the opportunity to be detraumatized. Ramazani Kakozi speaks of teaching youth, women, and others in the South Kivu province of Congo before they get caught up in violent movements. Pascal Tshisola Kulungu describes how the church in Congo was able to address tribal separations that existed within the church itself. Harold Miller portrays the peace efforts in the Sudan. Nora Musundi of Kenya tells about a prayer group that grew into an impressive national movement to address violence in Kenya.

Part V has the title, "Stories of Peacemaking in the Public Square." Toma Ragnjiya opens the chapter with a discussion of the complex interplay of political, tribal, and religious forces that shape the relationships between Christians and Muslims in Nigeria. He proceeds to recommend ways in which the common good can be addressed. Siaka Traore recounts the remarkable story of how a whole country entered into a process of repentance to avoid a civil war. Cecile Nyiramana describes working at de-traumatization across religious and tribal separations. Scott Holland's interpretation of the prophet Jeramiah's counsel to the Jewish exiles in Babylonian to "Seek the peace of the City," sparked continuing discussion during the Watu Wa Amani conference.

Part VI speaks of "The Courage to Hope." Watu Wa Amani conference sermons by Oliver Kisaka Simiyu, Matthew Abdulahi Gali, Million Belete, Steven Magnana, Mkodo Boseka, Bruce Khumalo, and Abraham Wuta Tizhe address the spiritual sources of hope amid violence. Fernando Enns speaks of "Peace, Healing, Forgiveness, and Renewal" available through faith in Jesus Christ. Toma Ragnjiya looks at "The Way Ahead."

Sidebars to the narratives give brief reactions, prayers, and responses to the stories recounted here. The Afterword relates the stories from Watu Wa Amani to the themes of the Decade to Overcome Violence as understood by Deenabandhu Manchala, Program Executive of Faith and Order (WCC). Appendix I gives the historical background to the World Council of Churches' Decade to Overcome Violence and the ongoing discussions with the Historic Peace Churches. Appendix II is the message from the Watu Wa Amani conference to the churches of the world, Appendix III contains a list of participants, and Appendix IV reproduces the conference program.

The editors thank all those who participated in the Watu Wa Amani conference for their valuable contributions. Many participants endured long, uncomfortable travel to be present. Those asked to make presentations, tell their stories, and lead worship services gave serious attention to their preparations and spoke from their hearts about many difficult things. In turn there were African congregational and denominational church leaders who helped the delegates attend but were not able to attend themselves. We thank the staff of Africa Quaker Vision (AQUAVIS), particularly John Muhanji, Lotan Migaliza, and Samson Ababu, who served as onsite managers and without whom the conference could not have take place. We thank the staff of the Brackenhurst International Conference Center for making last minute adjustments to accommodate the conference and for providing their excellent facilities and prompt attention to all the needs of the conference.

We thank Bethany Theological Seminary and its staff for providing a great many essential services for the conference, including the management of the funds, secretarial services for the convenor of the planning committee, and a venue for numerous planning sessions. We thank those who had the difficult job of translating the presentations between French and English. Particularly we thank the French departments of Manchester College and Earlham College for permitting Janina Traxler, Aletha Stahl, and Wendy Matheny to attend the conference and give many hours to the translation process.

We are very grateful to the donors who gave generously to support the travel costs of African participants. We thank the Plowshares Program for funding the visual and oral recording of this conference so that the materials can be available for research. We thank Dean Johnson and Ed Cundif for developing a DVD from the conference that can be used in churches around the world. We also thank the planning committee: Robert Herr, Judy Zimmerman Herr, Fernando Enns, Ann Riggs, Ben Richmond, Lon Fendall, Dean Johnson, Scott Holland, and Donald Miller, who gave much effort over three years to the planning of the conference.

Watu Wa Amani carried the conversation between the ecumenical community and the peace church tradition into the African churches. Our hope and prayer is that these conversations will continue both in Africa and the rest of the world and contribute to the birth of a peaceful Africa. We hope that they will also deepen the on-going conversation between the Historic Peace Churches and our partner churches from other traditions within the one ecumenical movement.

—*Donald Miller*
  Richmond, Indiana

INTRODUCTION

THE THEME OF THIS VOLUME is making peace theology relevant to the challenges of conflict in Africa. For such a time as this the peace churches are considering Africa as Africans have been making a stronger commitment to reconciliation and rebirth. We as Africans believe there is going to be change in the twenty-first century. In fact, the meetings from which this volume emerged were held in a nation that has been characterized as the most hopeful on the continent. After so many cycles of misgovernance and misappropriation of resources, we have begun to see light at the end of the tunnel.

We welcome this discussion at a time when we have not long ago-experienced and celebrated the peace protocols for the Sudan. In Kenya there were services of celebration for this breakthrough in the Sudanese peace effort. There were worship celebrations in Uganda and in many other places, including the United States. We have also seen some positive developments toward reconciliation in the Great Lakes, and for that we also thank God. We are experiencing a change of heart between Ethiopia and Eritrea, despite the challenges. Of course, we know that inter-religious councils have been working tirelessly in Sierra Leone and in Liberia to transform their nations into peaceful, sustainable societies.

But having highlighted a few of the signs of hope, it is also true that violence continues to threaten, to injure, and to kill people of all ages. We have low intensity violence, high intensity violence, and increased domestic violence. Even as a body of Christ we are fragmented, we are broken, we are in pain, and we are hurting. And so the challenge of violence has not only been with Christians since the time of Christ, but it is very much alive with us today. While it is true that violence is embedded in the ethos of our time, there is a growing awareness that the cycle of violence must be broken to protect life. As the churches on this continent have been wrestling and struggling to find meaningful ways to address the different forms of violence, we are joining hands with believers everywhere engaged in this great enterprise. We are part of the larger, international, universal church, joining in the search of peace.

A few years ago, some of us participated in the Eighth Assembly of the World Council of Churches. This was not only a time to reflect, but a time to redefine the goals and objectives of the pilgrimage of the churches worldwide. During this assembly, the churches committed themselves to seek reconciliation and peace under the banner of the Decade to Overcome Violence. This is a journey already started by Africans, and we have been asking the world church to journey with us. I recall when the presiding bishop of the Methodist Church in South Africa, Stanley Mogoba, thanked the ecumenical movement for the support that the churches and the peoples of South Africa had received in combating apartheid. He reminded us that the struggle was far from over. He appealed to the churches and the ecumenical movement to put new energy into the struggle against violence that has been wrecking our societies.

This decade devoted to overcoming violence will benefit from the rich tradition of Christian theological thinking, especially from the work done on biblical interpretation and ecclesiology. I am thrilled with the stories in this volume. We are a continent that has been bombarded by high level peace approaches, the United Nations types, the secular types. Meanwhile, the church has been struggling to anchor itself theologically. So for us as Christians it will be very helpful to be part of this reflection process because we believe that we need a fresh look at Christology. In our stories and in the experience of the churches in the conflict areas, there has been an emerging theological process that has not been fully captured and understood.

For instance, if you go to the Dinka churches in Sudan, you will experience a fresh theology and a new living out of that theology. The African church is struggling with how to share its spiritual and theological resources on peace with the rest of the world. And so please let us be open; let us bring forth our experiences. Because overcoming violence is not just a matter of the churches' practice, but a deep challenge to our theology. If the churches look anew at the basic themes of their theology, they will notice that they have a unique message to bring to the violence-ridden world—the message of forgiveness, justification, healing, and reconciliation.

We have gone through forty years of economic development experience that has not drawn on the richness of Africa's spiritual resources. That process has eaten away at our ethical values, replacing them with secular values, emphasizing individualism and monetary profits at the expense of the communitarian ethics that Africans believe in. Today, the very secular institutions that are the proponents of these theories of development have recognized that the missing link in the success of these development efforts is spirituality. I believe it is the same in the field of peacemaking. So our challenge is to articulate a theology that can penetrate and percolate through the thinking of the centers of power. It should shape the thinking of the leaders who have for a long time refused to believe in this very critical component of human life.

So to all who read these stories, "Karibu," as we say in East Africa, you are welcome. Let's continue on this journey, a journey of hope, as we also look back at the experiences of our people in the past and the conflicts and tensions that are with us today. May God bless us on this journey.

—*Agnes Abuom (Kenya)*
  Past President of the World Council of Churches

Part I

MARKETPLACES WHERE AFRICANS THINK AND TALK ABOUT THE COMMON GOOD

*A presentation of the theme that
holds together the stories in this book about peacemaking*

1

SOKONI:
AT THE MARKETPLACE

Samuel Kobia (Kenya)

The following chapter is from Samuel Kobia, The Courage to Hope *(Geneva: WCC Publications, 2003), 191-194. Used by permission of the World Council of Churches.*

IN AFRICA, THE DEMOCRATIC PARADIGM does not exclude God as did the European Enlightenment, nor is it silent on the moral and spiritual dimensions of good governance. True democratic transformation and practice in African society goes hand in hand with spirituality. Here I refer to spirituality in its deepest meaning, not just pious religiosity. Only then does it carry with it new possibilities for an integrated and genuinely wholistic approach to human life. For Africans, it is the close connection between human experience, structures, and systems that yields an integrated understanding of the value of life. The various belief systems and philosophies in Africa remind us that we live in a moral universe nurtured by the web of life-giving and life-sustaining relationships among all beings that inhabit the earth, including the ancestral spirits. Life cannot be packaged as a commodity, nor is it subject to the logic of the market.

The web of relationships in the human community is preserved under the care and nourishment of institutions of affection such as the family, which includes what may be referred to as extended households which guarantee social and cultural continuity. At the heart of this moral cosmology is the principle of participation. It is this vision of interdependent participation that creates structures of inclusion and hospitality that make life whole. It is through participation that the dignity of every individual is affirmed. To be is to participate. Exclusion from meaningful participation in matters that vitally affect one's life renders one a non-person.

This understanding of interdependent participation is consistent with the relational values we attach to human events. The functionality of those events is dependent on the quality of relationships and values transmitted in their retelling. How could the vision of Jesus bring about a society that is deeply divided and segregated? The inclusion and caring of Jesus call forth a society in which even the most vulnerable in the community will have his or her dignity respected and affirmed.

In our view, *sokoni* provides the space within which this offering is possible (in Kiswahili, sokoni means literally "at the market-place"). It is similar to the idea of the "public square." But this concept is based on the traditional African market. In 1997, sokoni was used as the theme of the WCC's Justice, Peace, and Creation conference on the theology of life which was held in Nairobi. The word symbolizes the totality of community life and space. In the context of sokoni the church's social capital is to be offered to the most vulnerable in the society. Sokoni is a place of memory and a space of contemporary action. It is the common ground and means through which an alternative vision of life may be realized. Sokoni in itself is not an ideology; neither is it just a marketplace where people go to shop for new ideas.

Unlike virtual space, sokoni is real. Parallels may be drawn between cyber-markets or cyberspace (non-physical space), but the symbolism of the village market is not a space of chaos—with unco-ordinated, uncontrolled, and random flows of information. It is not confined to those who can afford computers and have the technical know-how for seeking out information. It is the sanctuary of life, the place of dialogue with the past and the future where new ideas are born.

In sokoni, Africa is again called to relearn the value and art of dialogue, a way of speech and action that brings peace and builds new relationships that can help "win-win" situations. It is a space to visualize, reclaim, and reconstruct authentic community with new skills and instruments of social analysis. In other words, sokoni is the space for radical expression of the search for an alternative vision that could save not only Africa but the whole world. In relating what is good, the capacity for hope is regained and faith in life is reaffirmed. Here the center, the periphery, and the margin may be redefined.

Sokoni offers a new way of thinking and doing theology. It is the arena through which theoretical discourse becomes *palaver*, a historical event, which touches people's hearts and transforms their understanding of the world. In a way, sokoni provides space for paradigm shifts in which the logic of the global system is questioned and redefined. In this regard, a new spirituality is gained that is broader and deeper than mysticism, piety, or religiosity, because it is centered on the intrinsic value of life itself.

Where do human beings in contemporary times, be it in Africa or elsewhere, find consolation, meaning, and fulfillment for their existence? Where are the sanctuaries? In liturgical or ecclesial terms, could sokoni be the place where human beings come to lament, proclaim, and elaborate on the theology and ethic of life? Is sokoni not a place full of the historical and political memory of the people who are custodians of the resources (earth, air, trees, and the spirits) bequeathed to them by God through their ancestors? Is it not a place where we are all invited to seek justice and find peace in one another?

Sokoni is not a building, but a place full of people drawn together by the unifying force of Christ. It is a place in which life abounds in plenty and people are happy, not because of what they have but because of what they give and receive as a community.

Sokoni is a real event in the lives of real people called into critical dialogue with life itself. And as a market it is not just a space filled with goods and enterprises. Sokoni is also a sanctuary, a place where history is constantly being made. It has become for us the rebirth and renewal of the human spirit. Doing theology in the marketplace of life and in the presence of the community encourages one to bridge the gap between reflection and action. The world is full of markets, and so sokoni can be found everywhere. Therefore, theology can be done everywhere and at all times!

Sokoni is not just a physical market, open to the traffic of goods. Sokoni is ecu-space, an ecumenical space and a sanctuary for ideas. The concept itself is part of the process of paradigm shift, an authentic alternative vision of life, not just for Africa but for the world.

That is also the essence of the World Council of Churches' "Special Focus on Africa Programme" as a contribution to the reconstruction of Africa. We are called not just to react to the plight of Africa. We must not deplore Africa's present in terms of its marginality and human sadness that come with war and the anguish of poverty. We must not forever remain infected by nostalgic memories of the past in our desperation for solutions. Nor can we resort to the rigor of historicism lest we become victims of the ideological fatigue that characterize the end of an era. Rather, we must regard the recurrent problems in our world as an invitation to a new moment of enthusiasm (*enthusiasmos* = "God" within us, coming to life) which will bring to birth a new spirit coming first from Africa and then being offered to the rest of the world.

Sokoni must provide the space and opportunity for a new and lasting incarnation of the spirit so that those who are "infected" by it can spread the necessary enthusiasm for a new life to begin. Sokoni has the potential to become a space full of life-giving resources, a place where the goodness of life itself sanctifies our memory and connection with history.

A CONFERENCE WITH A DIFFERENCE?
PATSON NETHA (ZIMBABWE)

What a conference with a difference! There were times of excitement, times of laughter, and serious times when we could hear what different people are experiencing. We heard what is happening in the lives of the people from upper Africa right down to the southern part of Africa, the difficulties and the differences that are taking place. So much richness is involved in the Historic Peace Churches and in what they are doing. We were hearing from Nigeria about being involved with the Muslims.

Then we came to people involved in governments like in Burkina Faso, getting the whole nation in a stadium to hear the message of reconciliation, and even to the president himself addressing the nation on forgiveness. How rich is this! It was really rich when I listened to it. What a powerful thing that the peace churches are doing in addressing what's happening in their countries and in being involved to bring peace, healing, reconciliation.

It seems that everybody is working in his own corner. There are no networks in place to draw us together. If there were, that could be powerful, that could change our continent.

CHRISTIAN PEACEMAKING AND THE COMMON GOOD

Agnus Abuom (Kenya)

WORKING FOR PEACE MEANS WORKING for the common good. That may seem obvious, but our discourse and our actions do not always demonstrate this truth. Let me give you an example. For some time the Electoral Commission of Kenya (ECK) has been mandated to do civic education. In 2003 we had an evaluation of the impact of this program of civic and voter education. Our major finding was that most Kenyans, if not all, are very well informed. They know who they should vote for, but the frustrating thing is that they have not adjusted their voting patterns to fit with their knowledge and wisdom. I was asked to help the electoral commission in designing a program to educate voters in ways that their voting fits their values.

The same point can be made about our faith. Most of us Christians know how we ought to act to be faithful to our Creator. We know our history. We know what the ancestors have entrusted us with. But the challenge we face today is translating our faith into reality, into actions.

As we think about the threats to peace, we should consider the wisdom of the Nigerian writer, Chinua Achebe, in his book *Things Fall Apart*. Achebe argued that things were falling apart and the center was no longer holding. For me that center is the common good. If you enter the traditional African house, the little space where we live, there is a center pole that holds the dwelling together. And what is this common good to which we are called to be faithful?

When I look at the ecumenical movement, I see men and women who are giving their lives to restoring the common good that has been threatened over the centuries. I think of the Faith and Life movement that has been concerned about unemployment, about oppression of the poor people within their communities, and about persecution over the centuries. In fact, in the discussions at the World Council of Churches, much of the focus has been on war and on weapons. There has been lots of discussion about whether particular wars are just or not. In the WCC Central Committee meeting at Potsdam in 2001, there was debate about whether violence was justified for humanitarian purposes. The struggle between "just war" and pacifism continues, and at the center of this discussion has been the dilemma about the poor who are unable to defend themselves. Is just war the answer to this dilemma or is pacifism?

We've participated in the discussions about human rights which today we in the Christian family call "the struggle for human dignity." One of the most critical opportunities for witness among the churches of Latin America has been in situations in which people were under very dictatorial regimes. And of course there have been many such situations in Africa, such as Zimbabwe.

There have been discussions in the ecumenical movement about justice, peace, and the integrity of the creation, focusing especially on the threats to creation. It has become more apparent to us that the very center of human life, creation itself, is threatened. In some of these discussions, we have talked about creating a theology of life, because life is the most basic of common goods. This is the common good that calls us to be faithful to Christ, that demands we go out there in the public arena and speak to the forces of death.

It means creating, enhancing, facilitating, and protecting safe spaces for everybody. It means to be present, to participate, and to be heard. Safe space has become a scarce commodity in our world today. Here in Africa we say that the public space is occupied by two elephants that are fighting—and the grass, the common people, gets trampled. When the elephants are fighting, suffering people have no voice. They have no way of influencing the policies and activities that impact their lives.

To be faithful to the common good is also to celebrate the diversity of human gifts that provide the building blocks for the common good. Diversity is central to being human. Today we talk about different types of identities as a threat to the common good. There are tribal affiliations, gender identity, and religious affiliations. Political parties are often very ethnocentric. Even in the church we must celebrate and nurture diversity. So recognizing and acknowledging the pluralism of gifts is crucial for us.

Another way to understand the concept of the common good is to celebrate the unique gifts particular people bring to the human family. The giving and receiving of gifts is crucial in African cultures. We give and receive very special gifts at different moments of our lives. We who are Christians have received from Christ the good news, the transforming power of the Holy Spirit. But we tend to want to hold on to these gifts. Or we want to give them only on our own terms. One of the sad stories about our faith is that we guard our faith in the same way we hang on to our possessions. We take pride in our own denominations as the best and consider the others not so good.

I think that through their humanitarian work the churches have really been trying to help the poor. But we must ask whether the management of the institutions that we create is being done for the common good. Some churches have not done well in giving space for women. We are taught in the Gospels that we are not to give preference to Jew nor Gentile, male nor female. Yet we still have much discrimination in our churches. We must identify the gifts of all our people and let those gifts be used for the common good. That means recognizing God's image in every human being, acknowledging God's power to transform people, engaging faith communities to lift up the common good that promotes justice and peace.

I'm looking at common good on both an individual and collective basis. Some have thought that Africans don't really care for the individual, since we put so much emphasis on the community. However, we believe that the individual finds identity and meaning in community, and the community finds meaning and identity in the individual. So we intend for the common good to influence policies, to improve the common welfare of the people.

I want to challenge us as Historic Peace Churches to treasure the spirituality of Africans, both that of Christians and those of other faiths. African spirituality operates on the basis of affection for one another as in the early church. I cannot save large sums of money in the bank when my brother's children are not able to go to school.

At our best, we Africans operate on the economy of sufficiency and not greed. We place great emphasis on hospitality. When you come to my house, I will make you a meal. I used to go to a mission station where the missionaries would talk to the local people only through a window. You were not allowed in unless you had an appointment. This is not what we mean by "common good."

So as the African theologians continue to construct our theology, and as the African people continue reconstructing our societies, we call upon the Historic Peace Churches in Africa to come to the public square with your own integrity to influence those processes. We call upon you to be part of these discussions so that you can remain faithful to the calling of our Lord Jesus Christ. We need to build a society that is like a web, connected, relating to one another, caring for one another, like the early church. We need to bring back those values into the public arena for the common good so the center of human culture can hold firm. When the elephants are too powerful, we can still influence those elephants so that the grass will not continue to suffer.

Part II

HERITAGE OF PEACEMAKING

*An overview of the histories and heritages
that have shaped the Historic Peace Churches in Africa*

3

A FOUNDATIONAL THEOLOGY OF PEACEBUILDING

Paulus Widjaja (Indonesia)

THE BIBLICAL UNDERSTANDING OF PEACE

As members of Historic Peace Churches, we are proud to be perceived by other churches as forerunners in peacebuilding. We feel honored when, amid so many conflicts and wars in the world, other churches turn to us to ask for our wisdom. Yet we often assume too much about our understanding of this part of our theology. My hope is to encourage us to ponder in our minds and hearts the questions of whether and how far we really take seriously our claim as peace churches.

When we read the Bible, we soon find that there is no fixed definition of what the word *peace* means. In the Old Testament the word occurs 235 times and is used in many different contexts. Sometimes the word is used simply to ask about the condition or well-being of a person (Gen. 29:6; 43:23; 1 Sam. 29:7), a group of people (Jer. 15:5), animals (Gen. 37:14), and even war (2 Sam. 11:7). People at the time might have asked, "How's the peace of the war?" or "How is the peace of the animal?." But sometimes the word was used in a more serious context, such as in relation to worship, laws, politics, etc. (Num. 6:24-26; Lev. 26:6). So, it is impossible to find an exact definition of the word *peace*. What we can do is capture the nuances of meaning in the word.

A careful look at the various uses of the word peace in the Bible will show us that it covers a wide range of meanings. Peace is not understood in the Bible as simply the absence of war, or the absence and reduction of violence, or the transformation of conflict without violence. The biblical meaning of peace covers much more than that. If we look carefully at the Bible, there are at least three, possibly four, definitions of peace.

First, peace refers to the *well-being and material prosperity* signified by the presence of physical well-being and the absence of war, disease and famine (Jer. 33:6,9). Second, peace refers to *just relationships* signified by right relationships among people, nations, and social groups, where there is no oppression or exclusion in whatever form (Isa. 54:13-14). Third, peace also refers to the *moral integrity* of the person; here there is straightforwardness and no deceit, fault, or blame (Ps. 34:13-14).

In the New Testament, we find yet another nuance to the word peace. It is also related to *God and the good news from God*. This is where we get the expression "God of Peace," (Rom. 15:13, 16:20; 2 Cor. 13:11; 1 Thess. 5:23; 2 Thess. 3:16; and Heb. 13:20).

As we look at these various meanings, we conclude that peace in the Bible is related to the *wholeness* of human beings and all creatures. It is related to the *physical, relational, moral* as well as *spiritual* dimensions of humankind. If we happen to be in a place where there is no war around us, we can not simply say, "This is good, there is peace here." If we would like to see peace, we need to understand that peace is related to many dimensions of human life. Perhaps there is no war; but where there is social and economic oppression, there is no peace. Perhaps we do not have conflict with our neighbors, but if within our self is deception, there is no peace.

A PEACE CONTINUUM

Peace is related to many dimensions of human life. So if we are engaged in peacebuilding, we should not be satisfied with only one dimension of peace. Peacebuilding takes place on many levels. Understanding peace as a continuum may help us get involved with peacebuilding. The continuum starts from humans' peace with God and extends to peace with their enemies. This continuum helps each of us get involved with peacebuilding, because each of us can judge ourselves to see at what level we are already comfortable, then strive for the next level. Someone might say it's very hard for us to love our enemies. But people who find it hard to love enemies can still be involved in other levels of peacebuilding. So everyone can be involved at some level. Peacebuilding should start with peace with God. In training I have done in peacebuilding and conflict transformation, I have met people from many different religions and backgrounds. This principle has been confirmed again and again. Many people admit that the horror of war and community conflict is so great that they often feel torn apart by what they see and hear on the field, even as they work for peace. Therefore they have said, "Without peace with God, we cannot talk about peacebuilding, let alone to do peacebuilding." So peace is not something that is built outside and only then comes inside. No, it is the other way around. Peace always starts from within, and only then ripples out.

Peace starts with peace with God; but God, the source of peace, is also the God who wills peace for all creation. God does not want us to stay at the first level of peace with God. He wants us to move forward to the next levels. We see this clearly in Jesus Christ, who demonstrated the way of peace. Jesus did not talk only about peace with God but also about peace with families, peace with neighbors, and so on until we come to the most difficult part, peace with enemies. This is indeed difficult for us, especially if we have been hurt by people we then perceive as enemies.

This should not discourage us from getting involved with peacebuilding, because between the two poles—peace with God and peace with enemies—there are many forms of peacebuilding:

- peace with our own selves. Are we satisfied and content with ourselves?
- peace with our families, whether nuclear or extended families;
- peace with our sisters and brothers in Christ in the local church;
- peace with our sisters and brothers in Christ from other churches;
- peace with people of other faiths;
- peace with our neighbors;
- peace with colleagues at work;
- peace with other citizens (peace within the nation);

• peace with citizens of other countries (peace between nations).

EMPOWERMENT FOR PEACEBUILDING

Another question is how we empower Christians to do such peacebuilding. There are at least two basic disciplines that we need to consider: the discipline of *discernment* and the discipline of *radical Christ-like living*.

I will start with the discipline of *discernment*. We need to be alert to the conditions around us to see whether there is peace in all areas of society. We may not have war in our neighborhoods or in our personal contacts, but we should determine whether all the other dimensions of peace are present.

As Christians, we need to realize that our confession of the lordship of Christ is a claim about the cosmos, the entire created order. This means that all of the areas of human life are under the lordship of Christ; there is no reality in the world that is not. There is no substantial dichotomy between Christ and culture, creation and redemption; there is no socio-economic-political realm that can be avoided by the church and Christians and left alone to be governed by its own values and norms. We have talked about holistic and comprehensive peace. So we cannot say "Oh, peace is not our business" or "Peace is our business, but it is only among those at church." To confess that Jesus Christ is our Lord means that everything in the world is under the lordship of Christ.

So we have to be engaged. And even though we have a positive attitude toward the world, we nevertheless need clear criteria for judging whether historical events are the work of God or the work of the devil, whether such events bring about peace or evil. From the life and death of Jesus Christ we get the criteria we need. And the body of Christ, the church, is the discerning community in which Christians listen together for God's will for the world. In and through the church, we discern God's work in our history and reflect on whether or not a historical event is consistent with the meaning of Christ. If we see the meaning of Christ in a historical event, then we can confirm it. But if we do not see it, then we can confront it. So this is the kind of peacebuilding on which we can work. We have to discern all dimensions in our life, using the criteria Jesus has given us, to judge what is happening in the world and what to confirm or to confront.

A second discipline we need to develop is *radical Christ-like living*. As human beings, we are created with the capabilities of imagination and creativity. But we also have limitations, and therefore we need to be humble and discipline ourselves. So we cannot simply say, "Because I have been created in the image of God, therefore I will be a good person. I will be peaceful." No, it doesn't work that way. We have capabilities, but we also have limitations. And because we have limitations, we prefer to follow our own rather than God's desires. We need to be fully intentional, forming our Christian character so that we become more like Christ (Rom. 8:29, 12:2; Gal. 4:19; Phil. 2:5; 2 Cor. 3:17-18).

Such discipline has become more important because, since the time of Constantine, the church has shifted focus from concrete actions to philosophical and doctrinal matters. If we look at the catechetical materials we use to prepare church members, we find doctrines about who God is, who Jesus is, the nature of the Trinity, and so forth. It all has to do with philosophical doctrines. We have moved our teaching too far from concrete actions of faithfulness to Christ.

We must remind ourselves that faith is not *gnosis* (knowledge) but a way of living in faithfulness to God (Rom. 8:5-6; Gal. 5:13-17). Such a way of life involves all aspects of our lives, including our beliefs, values, commitments, orientation, and faith practices. Faithful living reflects the existential meaning of life manifested in the acts and behaviors that form our way of life, so there is a consistency between our internal convictions and the external manifestations of that awareness in our daily lives. If we believe in something, it should also be manifested outwardly. In other words, if we make peace our way of life, all aspects of our life will be oriented toward peace. There will be consistency between what we believe about peace and the concrete peaceful behavior we show in our daily lives.

For the two disciplines outlined above to become reality, we need to take at least two important paths into peace as believers: *empowerment of individuals* and *empowerment of structures*.

I want to start with the empowerment of individuals. How can we develop the character of the individuals so they become peacebuilders? Becoming peacebuilders is not something that can happen automatically. We have to do something to help individual Christians become peacebuilders, to become like Christ. So we need to look at the curriculum material we use in the church, to be sure it adequately prepares adults and children alike with the insights and skills necessary for peacebuilding. What are the church members reading? Are there enough materials to help people prepare talks about peace and peacebuilding? Are there enough materials to equip our church members so they can become peacebuilders?

We also need to ask whether we have made peace central in our worship. Do we have a peace month or peace Sunday in our church calendar? Do we organize prayer and fasting for peace? Do we plan pilgrimages for peace? What about peace education in the church and Christian schools? Again, is there enough programming and material there that we actually help individuals become peacebuilders? Such are the questions we need to ask. We also need to ask if we provide training in nonviolent conflict transformation for our pastors, elders, deacons, and even ordinary church members.

In my experience with peacebuilding, I have found that Muslims participate more often than Christians. It may be that Christians assume that peace is central to our gospel, since Jesus put so much emphasis on it. Yet too few church conflicts are solved nonviolently. In Indonesia, for example, thirty percent of the cases in the Supreme Court are related to church conflicts. Thirty percent! This shows our shortcomings in putting theology into action.

Besides the empowerment of individuals, we must also talk about the empowerment of our structures. We must ask if we have mechanisms in the church to solve and transform conflicts inside and outside the church. Many churches simply assume that we can deal with church conflicts nonviolently. They assume that Christlike peacemaking will take place. But that is often not the case. We must set up mechanisms in the church so when conflicts arise people know what they are going to do and where to get help.

If we have youth committees, women's committees, missions committees, and worship committee, do we also have peace committee in charge of the education and training of church members in peacebuilding inside and outside the church? And if we have such committees, are they able to function as mediators to transform the conflicts in church and society nonviolently?

So there are many things we need to do. Yes, some are difficult. We need to train ourselves, we need good discipline, we need to gain knowledge and skills. But, some are ordinary things any of us can do. So whatever situation we are facing, peacebuilding is not simply a dream. It is a concrete vision we can achieve. The vision of the psalmist should also become ours. We should envision a situation where "Loving kindness and truth have met together; Righteousness [justice] and peace have kissed each other" (Ps. 85:10). This is a vision we too can achieve. Mercy, truth, justice, and peace can and must embrace each other. This is not simply a dream.

CRUCIAL ISSUES FOR THE CHURCHES
FERNANDO ENNS (GERMANY)

Discussions in the African context disclose several topics that are particularly crucial and will be on the future agenda of the Historic Peace Churches as well as of the World Council of Churches. One is the relationship between different faith groups, especially the relationship between Muslims and Christians. A second one is the question of security. In addition, and underlying all questions of violence and nonviolence, are the economic problems and poverty. What is the role of the church in the public sphere? Here we will have to discuss with others the defense of human rights to create sustainable and just peace within society. Will the churches be able to inform their societies that these rights are based on core Christian values, and do we ourselves believe that they need to be grounded in a spirituality and theology communicable to non-Christians? For Christians, human rights are more than just a humanistic idea.

By entering the public sphere we run the risk of getting our hands dirty. That is a new thing for some members of the peace churches. It is one thing to create separate communities where you live at a distance from the broader society and try to be a sign of hope within that society by being different. Historically this has been the way of the peace churches. The African context shows that this is not enough. It is time to move into the public sphere and become much more involved. You cannot be a church in Africa without dealing with HIV/AIDS, dealing with the question of how to defend human rights, dealing with economic imbalance and right governance. The mission of the church to be the advocate for the poor and an ambassador of reconciliation will inevitably lead to the public sphere. Peace churches in Africa are beginning to realize this. And this experience is something that people from other contexts need to learn from our sisters and brothers in the African church.

4

THE HERITAGE OF FRIENDS PEACEMAKING IN AFRICA

Malesi Elizabeth Kinaro (Kenya)

QUAKERS BELIEVE IN THE PRIESTHOOD of ordinary people like me. So although I am not a minister in the normal sense of the word, I trust I can make a contribution to this volume by writing about the Friends church in Africa, beginning with a historical background and then discussing some of the peacemaking efforts of Friends in Kenya. I will refer to "Friends" and "Quakers" interchangeably in my comments. The term *Friends* comes from John 15, in which Jesus calls us his friends if we obey his commands. The term *Quaker* was one given to Friends by those who noticed that Friends were so moved by the ministry of the Holy Spirit in their lives that they trembled physically.

We Friends are very diverse. You will find among Friends a variety of beliefs, organizational patterns, and worship styles. The Friends worship groups in Kenya begin with village meetings (in some countries called preparatory meetings), monthly meetings, and quarterly meetings. In Kenya we also have regional meetings and these together form yearly meetings. We refer to them as meetings to make it clear that we don't consider these gatherings of believers to be the church. They each constitute a small part of the body of Christ, the church. And of course, Friends are only part of that larger body.

Among the Quakers there are two basic types of worship. First are what we call "unprogrammed meetings." In unprogrammed

44

meetings, people wait in silence upon God, without relying on the spoken word from a trained minister. The meeting for worship may be completely silent from the beginning to the end. Or someone might sing or speak or minister or read from the Bible or an inspirational book, as the Holy Spirit leads. Among the congregations that are unprogrammed you have people who are Christ-centered, who believe in all the things other people believe about Christ. Others are liberal theologically and believe in many things, especially that God speaks to people through any religion, any place. You might also have those who are universalists, who do not believe in the divinity of Jesus. I have met some who are almost atheists. The unprogrammed meeting is the original mode of Quaker worship with roots in nineteenth-century Britain.

The second type of Friends meeting is what we call the "programmed meeting." Programmed meetings originated in the United States and came to Africa through the missionaries who served here from 1902. Programmed meetings are like most other churches in having a definite worship program that typically includes singing, Scripture reading, and messages or sermons. For some Friends churches in the United States this might mean a carefully planned worship program, but in Africa we are more flexible and spontaneous. Along with this style of worship, programmed meetings among the Friends are almost always centered in Christ. Some programmed Friends have pastors who have been trained in seminary or Bible college, but the worship services in our Friends churches in Kenya are most often led by lay people, and the pastors concentrate on giving spiritual guidance.

Friends have many organizations, perhaps more than other Christian movements. I will concentrate on the groups that involve Quakers in Africa, since it would be too complicated to talk about Friends organizations globally. We have the Friends World Committee for Consultation, whose headquarters is in London and whose Africa office is in Nairobi. Their work is to do what the names say—consult. They put Friends in touch with each other. Then we have the American Friends Service Committee (AFSC), headquartered in Philadelphia. They have offices in several parts of Africa. The AFSC is involved in development, humanitarian efforts, and peace and justice work of many kinds.

The Friends United Meeting is the mother body that brought Quakerism to Kenya about a century ago. Evangelical Friends International, on the other hand, is the mother body of most of the Friends churches in the Great Lakes Region: Rwanda, Burundi, and Congo. We have other Quaker bodies like the Quaker Peace and Social Witness, based in Britain. There is the Quaker United Nations Organization, with offices in New York and Geneva. Then we have the Friends Committee on National Legislation, which is in Washington, D.C., and deals with the political, economic, and social issues in the United States as well as around the world.

We have the group called Right Sharing of World Resources, which supports income-generating projects. Other groups like Friends Peace Teams give support to the African Great Lakes Initiative to do development and peace work in Africa. We have the Quaker Violent Conflict Prevention Network, which in Africa is shortened to Quaker Peace Network (QPN). Formed recently, it brings together all the Quaker peace organizations, and they are seeking to influence national and global policies in the direction of peace. They are asking how the organizations at the local level can help the organizations that are at the policy level to do their work better.

Friends are found in many parts of Africa. Quakerism came to South Africa in 1728, when two Dutch Quakers started a worship meeting that eventually became a monthly meeting. In 1949 Quakers in South Africa formed a yearly meeting. The Quakers in this part of Africa are unprogrammed. Quaker missionaries from the United States came to Kenya in 1902. Today Friends in Kenya make up the largest Quaker community in the world, numbering between 150,000 and 200,000 members, and they are organized into fourteen yearly meetings. Kenyan Friends carried out evangelism in Uganda beginning in 1946, and Uganda became a yearly meeting in 1979. Friends also began evangelistic work in Tanzania in 1962 and by 1980 Tanzania became a yearly meeting.

Some of the Quakers who had started the mission in Kenya went on to found the Friends church in Burundi in 1934. Burundi Friends in turn evangelized people in the Eastern part of Congo. Then, when missionaries were expelled from Burundi in the early 1980s, some began establishing churches and schools in Rwanda. So there are many Quakers in the three major East African countries—Kenya, Uganda, and Tanzania—as well as in what we now call the Great Lakes region.

As we begin to look at peace efforts among Friends in Africa, we have to admit that the conflicts in Africa reflect poorly on us, since there is such a high percentage of Christians in East and Central Africa. When violence begins, it's hard to believe that so many people are Christians, because the conflict goes on despite people's faith affiliations. So Quakers in East Africa have concentrated on local projects that focus on the needs of people. We consider peacemaking one of the discipleship tools, central to what the church does. This has not always been the case and has not been easy. The early missionaries to these parts felt that peace was an integral component of evangelism and did not require special stress. This left out a major tradition of who Friends are. We are reclaiming this heritage so Friends and those with whom they come in contact are equipped with the peacemaking skills so crucial in our continent, where violent conflict is rampant.

When I was involved in peace work in Burundi in 1993, some of the Friends I worked with were worried. They told me, "Our emphasis is on evangelism. When you bring in peace work, people will begin to get confused. Because Jesus is the Prince of Peace, if we help people to know Christ, they will know peace." But now as the conflicts in Africa have continued, people have begun to realize that knowing Christ internally isn't enough. Sometimes we Africans are accused of having a Christianity that is only skin deep. Speaking for Friends at least, I think that has changed. Friends from many countries in Africa have come to understand that to follow Christ completely is to become serious about peacemaking.

Among the questions that should be asked are these: What does being a Christian mean to a poor African person? Does it mean that if I become a Christian I will get a better education, or get some material support? Has our faith taken root? Before the missionaries came we had our own beliefs as Africans. Christianity was brought in and we were told to adopt different ethics and lifestyles. Many people changed and began to practice Christian values, but before they got rooted, liberal theology came in. The people who were trying to help us understand Christianity were themselves confused. Before we could root ourselves in a true Christian ethic, we were being given a theology that was very unclear.

We are in a unique position. We are in the agrarian age, and at the same time we are in the electronic age. We are expected to understand electronics, to know the realities in which we live. We are supposed to know about the Internet and cyberspace, yet we are still making our houses from mud and cow dung. Have those who say African Christianity is only skin deep ever imagined what it is like to be in this situation? What makes syncretism so common in Africa?

There are many issues that we really need to think about. I remember reading a book about the war in Rwanda. The victims of ethnic violence there were shocked that the members of their own congregations were killing them. We need to remember how crucial the loyalty to their tribes is for Africans. The bond is so strong that if our tribe is threatened, it is possible for some to forget all the Christian teachings as they defend their tribe. Meanwhile there are those whose testimony shines above tribal affiliations.

How can we use the tribal bond without its being destructive? Let us not forget how very, very strong culture is for some of us in Africa. I know of young men in Kenya who have married widows whose husbands have died from AIDS because that is what their culture says they must do. They know they are going to die from the AIDS infection carried by the widows but say, "I would rather die than get the curse of my brother's spirit." And there are young girls who get married to widowers they know are HIV-positive. They tell you they would rather die honorably as somebody's wife than remain single and become a laughingstock, some kind of outcast.

How can we deal with terrible consequences of some of our cultural practices? How can we make our theology more relevant amid tribal war? An African theologian has written that Africans are notoriously religious, as if that were bad. When we make fun of who we are spiritually, we are in danger of losing the force of our convictions.

In our peacemaking efforts in Africa, we are trying to help church people understand political systems, so that they are not just driven along by tribal emotions. We are working to help individuals understand themselves and how they react to things. As we saw in Rwanda, we are all capable of being murderers. Some of us are involved in peace work that affirms the individual and helps the individual to affirm others. Most are involved in counseling and conflict resolution. Some are doing trauma healing with war and HIV/AIDS victims. Some of us are working for economic empowerment so our poverty is not exploited. Some are looking at ways we can incorporate positive traditional peacemaking skills into Christian principles and practices.

And many of us are realizing that unless we build the capacities of the young people, the cycle will keep on repeating itself. The hope of changing this continent is based on helping the youth to think differently. The young people must be made to know the violent history of the continent through slavery, colonialism, and neo-colonialism that has affected our cooperate psyche. They must be made to understand that to remain here is to enslave ourselves. That we must consciously move from this psyche to one of positive development.

5

MENNONITES IN AFRICA

Komuesa Kalunga (Congo)

THE GENERAL THEME DEVELOPED HERE is "people of peace." The sub-theme I was asked to discuss was how, in historical and theological terms, the Mennonite church became a peace church. This chapter has three parts: first, the nature and mission of the church in the world; second, how historically and theologically we became a peace church; third, how as Congolese Mennonites we have understood peace.

To understand the nature and mission of the church, we need to define what the church is. I prefer to approach these two notions together: the church living in the world and the sign of the new world. Since the beginning, the church was called to be a community in which the kingdom of God was the determining reality. The church today is the presence of Christ in the world. This is true because the church possesses the word of God. The church is truly founded on that gospel, given though Jesus Christ. It participates in the future kingdom of God that is seen in Jesus Christ.

Evangelical communities underscore the idea that the mission of churches is to unite the people of God throughout the human community. The first task is to glorify God and to proclaim the salvation given only through Jesus Christ. The world is a mission field. All human beings must be called to conversion. Some excerpts of the declarations unifying these movements internationally state this vision. Salvation in Jesus Christ is offered without exception to all people who are not yet tied to Christ by faith.

The polar opposite to this first approach is a second approach which understands the mission of the church in the world as a collaboration to establish a society of peace, of fellowship, and of social justice. The church is not the church unless it serves others. To interpret this idea radically, the task of the church is to recognize the world's agenda. By itself the church has no meaning; its only mission is to bring about the human ideal proposed by Jesus Christ. The goal is not to hope for the worldwide establishment of Christianity and to perpetuate Christian imperialism and colonialism. Instead, Christianity must save the world and offer it a new perspective.

Most Protestant churches hope to avoid such extreme attitudes, which are caricatures of the church's mission in the world. For most Protestants the church should be a place of communion, of services, and of testimonies which vary from one context to another according to the specific challenges we are called to confront.

We can nevertheless note some theological options. The communion of believers cannot live by and for itself. It has neither its foundation nor its finality in and of itself. By becoming involved in daily reality, the church carries out the messianic work of Jesus Christ and takes part in God's story that we have in the world. In short, the church is called to be a sign of God's Word that the church proclaims. Such a conception of the church's mission in the world cannot be reduced to a collection of dogmas or doctrines. Any particular situation requires a new word and a new act as well as the creative faculties and attitudes of leaders. The mission of the church is to announce to the world its sanctification and its liberation.

Now we come to the second point: how the Mennonite church became a peace church. Everything started in the sixteenth century, when there was a major reform in the church. The fathers of this reform movement were Martin Luther and Ulrich Zwingli. Within the circle of Zwingli's friends, a major split developed. Some theological differences eventually set Zwingli against the younger reformers who surrounded him, especially concerning the question of baptism. Zwingli favored child baptism, but the other young reformers, especially Conrad Grebel and Felix Mantz, opposed the baptism of children. They argued that baptism should be offered only to those who had professed their faith as adults.

The rupture occurred during a meeting on January 17, 1525, organized by the Zurich city council. Zwingli allied himself with the city council. Grebel and his friends took a different position. On January 21, 1525, during a clandestine prayer session, a Catholic priest named Georges Blaurock asked to be rebaptized. The Mennonite church worldwide recognizes this date as the birth of the Anabaptist movement that formed the roots of the Mennonite church. Thereafter, the Anabaptists separated themselves from Zwingli.

In time the group who favored adult baptism was severely persecuted. Unfortunately for them something else happened in their theological circle. A man named Thomas Muntzer had also been preaching against child baptism. However his social ideology advocated violence, and he led the Peasant War in 1524-1525 in the province of Westphalia. This war was repressed with great bloodshed. Because of this event, those opposing child baptism were assumed to be associated with Thomas Muntzer. Historically, those who opposed child baptism were the reformers called Anabaptist, meaning they were convinced that those who were baptized as infants should be baptized again as adults.

There were different kinds of Anabaptism. Some were violent; others were enlightened or spiritualistic. At that time, a former priest named Menno Simons appeared, also a convert to Protestantism. He organized his own group, later called Mennonites after Simons' first name. They were given the name Mennonites to distinguish them from those who were violent and those who were charismatic or spiritualistic. From this point on what I say about Anabaptist refers particularly to those who follow the nonviolent teachings of Menno Simons.

In their theology of nonresistance to malice based on Matthew 5:39, the Anabaptists see two opposing leaders, two opposing kingdoms. The first is the Prince of Peace. The second is the Prince of Discord. The Prince of Peace is Jesus Christ. His kingdom is the kingdom of peace, which is his church. For Anabaptists, the local church provides an alternative. The true mission is to bring together all Christians, and the church should define itself by the cross, the cross which is a revelation, God's way of loving. The cross constitutes the difference between this pacifism and humanistic pacifism

To go back to the role the Anabaptists give to the prince of peace, the messengers are messengers for peace. The word of Christ is the word of peace; its reward is the reward and heritage of peace. For further insight, see Hebrews 7, Isaiah 9, Luke 1, and Romans 10. In light of the strong scriptural teaching on peace, I've never understood how Christians can justify by the Scriptures revenge, oppression, war, physical violence, slitting throats, killing people, looting, rape.

Menno Simons offered an answer. Here is what he said in 1539:

> Those who have new life do not wage war or become involved in fighting. They are children of peace, who have beat their swords into plowshares and do not know war. Because we should shape ourselves in Christ's image, our fortress is Christ. Our defense is our patience; our sword is the word of God. All the lances and other iron weapons—we leave them to those, alas, who consider human blood and animal blood to be of equal value.

Similarly, long before Menno Simons, Conrad Grebel said with respect to peace that the gospel and its followers are not to be protected by the sword. They should not worry about protecting themselves. Real Christians will not use the sword, a worldly weapon. They do not participate in war. For them, taking human life is forbidden.

That was the church's situation in the sixteenth century. Today we have many ideas concerning peace, in particular the theory of just war. This theory, which dates almost from the fourth century, was first formulated by the Roman philosopher Cicero. It was reiterated by Thomas Aquinas and before him St. Augustine. In essence this theory says that the leadership of the country has the right to defend the nation. Others emphasize that it is a response to extreme injustice, an injustice not only material but also moral, such as the violation of rights. Those who believe in just war say this theory applies only when all efforts to resolve conflict via negotiation have failed. War must be only a final option.

There are those who assert that Romans 13 teaches that it is necessary to obey the authorities, including their orders to participate in war. But when I read these chapters, I offer my own interpretation, not just an exegesis, but a personal reflection. This chapter of Romans, written by Paul, causes me to ask "Is it true that in Paul's time they had conscription?" The writings of that period indicate that the Roman army recruited only volunteers. I'm convinced the Scripture teaches that the authorities of a country are human authorities and as humans, inclined to sin. They can make laws and give orders which do not conform to God's will. So I believe we should not just follow Romans 13, but Acts 5:29, which says "We must obey God rather than any human authority."

How does the Mennonite Church of Congo understand the concept of peace? Often when we speak of peace, we refer to weapons and war, meaning that we have peace when there is no war, when people do not use weapons. But I think that we also have verbal violence; we attack people with hateful words. Violence can also be the oppression of the poor that pushes them to violence. In the Congo, despite all these difficulties, we have those who preach peace. At the university where I am a professor, we are in the process of setting up a department focused on conflict management and transformation. This is good, but I am afraid that peace remains the domain of intellectuals, who exist mostly in urban centers. The advocates for peace cannot easily go to the rural areas to preach. But at least we are trying.

I am pleased to be one who comes from a Historic Peace Church (Anabaptist-Mennonite) because in the sixteenth century we were already becoming a reform movement within a reform movement. When everyone was afraid of the state, the Mennonites had already defined a pathway for ourselves. That is a historical heritage that is also a theological heritage.

6

EKKLESIYAR YAN'UWA A NIGERIA

Filibus Gwama (Nigeria)

First of all, I admonish and urge that petitions, prayers, intercessions, and thanksgiving be offered on behalf of all men. For kings and all who are in a position of authority and high responsibility, that (outwardly), we may pass a quiet and undisturbed life (and inwardly) a peaceable one in all godliness and reverence and seriousness in every way.
—1 Timothy 2:1-2, Amplified Bible

Bless those who persecute you (who are cruel in their attitude toward you); bless and do not curse them. Repay no one evil for evil, but take thought for what is honest and proper and noble (aiming to be above reproach) in the light of God. If possible as far as it depends on you, live at peace with everyone.
—Romans 12:17-18, Amplified Bible

EKKLESIYAR YAN'UWA A NIGERIA (EYN or The Church of the Brethren in Nigeria) has about 160,000 members, organized in 44 district church councils, 402 local congregations, and over 1000 local church branches. The church was founded by Stover Kulp and Albert Helser in 1923. These two young men came from Church of the Brethren in America. They arrived in Lagos in 1922 and started work as missionaries at Garkida in Adamawa State on March, 17, 1923. Part of what is

54

now the EYN was founded by other mission bodies. Ashland Brethren came to Mbororo-Michika area in the early 1950s and later joined with the Church of the Brethren (COB) in Nigeria. Basel Mission started work in Gavva-Ngoshe area in 1959 by sending Rev. Werner Schoni from Switzerland. They joined COB in 1964.

Stover and Albert were sent on a trial mission in Western Borno among the Bura people. Borno was the first area to accept Islam in Nigeria. Before the coming of the British, the Borno Empire had existed for many years as the main power in the area. Through the Holy Jihad, they expanded Islam to a length of more than a hundred kilometers. Those who rejected Islam but wanted to remain in their lands were enslaved by the Muslims. Those who refused to be slaves to the Muslims fled into the mountains and remained there until the coming of the British government.

Through their system of indirect rule, the British imposed the Muslim rulers over the non-Muslim areas not because they respected Islam, but because that was the only way they thought they could make people pay taxes and have them work on the roads and anywhere else. Although the British and the Muslims had different interests, they worked together to exploit the non-Muslims. The British officers in Borno and the Muslim leaders deliberately created tension among the tribes, which they knew were difficult to control. They would create some problems between these tribes, which often would push them into war with one another, until both tribes became weak. Then, the Muslims with their British allies would intervene and take control of both tribes. This was the situation in which the first Church of the Brethren missionaries found themselves.

In the light of this situation it was not easy for them to establish their mission work in Biu area. Both the British officers and the emir of Biu (the Muslim leader) would not allow the mission work to start in Biu. But through a series of struggles with the British official in Borno and in Lagos (the Commissioner), it was finally agreed to let work start in Garkida. At that time Garkida was a place known for venomous snakes, scorpions, and many dangerous animals. Despite firm opposition from secular and religious groups, the Church of the Brethren Mission was started. The missionaries discovered that the people were in need of being saved from suffering such as disease, hunger, war, poor hygiene, illiteracy, and domination by Muslims.

The missionaries gave themselves for the gospel and for the people of Nigeria. They promoted the historical Brethren love feast with foot washing and a simple meal of the bread and cup, as well as the triune immersion mode of baptism for all believers. They emphasized simple living and tolerance for others. Of all the Brethren missionary teachings, the Church of the Brethren members in Nigeria value and cherish the heritage of the brotherly love more than anything else.

For reasons best known to themselves, the early missionaries did not emphasize other Brethren principles such as wearing a special garb, the holy kiss, and rejecting war. Their main concern was to make the Nigerians followers of Christ, not Brethren. Thus they focused their attention more on what the Bible said in the African context and not on denominational beliefs and practices.

Why did they not teach the Brethren beliefs and practices? Why did they ignore the peace position of the Church of the Brethren? Didn't they believe in the position of the Church? Yes, these missionaries believed in the tenets of the Church of the Brethren. Albert Helser, Stover Kulp and many others were conscientious objectors to war and therefore pacifist.

The truth is that, missionary churches were shaped by the situation in which the missionaries found themselves contextually, not by what the mother denomination believed. Thus it was not surprising that the brothers and sisters who went to preach the gospel in Nigeria established a church not fully dependent upon the Brethren beliefs and practices, but upon what they felt the Holy Spirit was leading them to do in a particular context.

The missionaries in Nigeria preached the gospel of reconciliation and love. The church established by Stover and Albert and many others who followed them was centered more on the love of God for humanity than on a doctrinal understanding of peace. It was the missionaries' conviction that once the message of God's love was planted in the hearts of the people, it would be natural for them to see the importance of peace. With sincerity and vigor they preached the gospel of love and reconciliation. The missionaries were able to reconcile the warring tribes and established a cordial relationship with them and the Muslim leaders.

Although the Brethren in Nigeria did not teach peace and pacifism according to the belief of the Brethren in the United States, their way of peacemaking was very practical. It was seen and understood by the believers and unbelievers alike. It was not a peace centered simply on evidence, but a peace deeper than external conflict. Christianity for them was a way of life, advocating the worth of the individual and the importance of home and family, which they believed was the way to peace and reconciliation.

The Brethren not only preached Christianity as a new way of life, they demonstrated it practically in their daily lives and their relationship with all people. They showed their witness to reconciliation through the practice of hospitality, in their care of patients at hospitals, in their rural health and education, agriculture programs, and anywhere they worked.

They demonstrated practically what it meant to be a Christian to such an extent that even those who once hated them, like the Emir of Biu, later regretted their hatred and eventually pressed to have the Brethren schools built at Waka, not far from his house. Some Muslims even sent their children to learn from the missionaries. What was even more amazing was the recognition of the Kulp Bible school by the Emir of Yola. For many years, and to this day, the Lamido of Adamawa has a high respect for the Church of the Brethren in Nigeria. During the time of the early missionaries, the Emir came to Kulp Bible school to inspect the farms and to visit the missionaries. The Emir trusted the missionaries completely.

For the Nigerian missionaries, peace was understood not primarily through preaching and teaching nonviolence, but through practical acts of loving and serving in life. Peace in the Nigerian context is to know Jesus Christ. Peace is to love God with your entire mind, with all your soul, and your neighbor as yourself. Peace is to be free from poverty, hunger, disease, ignorance, and domination. Peace is not the absence of war; instead it is a war against evil and injustice. Peace is the refusal to compromise with injustice, sin or evil acts. Peace is the courage to face evil in its all dimensions through the Spirit of God.

Stover Kulp and many other missionaries were skilled at facing reality and establishing good relationships among tribes. That was the reason Stover didn't want to stay in one place for a long time. He moved from Garkida to Dille, Dille to Lassa, and from Lassa to Mubi, teaching and preaching brotherly love and reconciliation.

As members of the Church of the Brethren in Nigeria (EYN) we claim with our fellow Brethren in United States that we are a peace church. In fact, even if we do not give voice to it, our relationship with the COB made us to be known in Nigeria as a peace church both by other Christians and by Muslims. The missionaries believed in the New Testament concept of peace, not in its specific historical interpretation, and so do we. They emphasized brotherly love as recorded in the New Testament without necessarily concentrating on things like war, pacifism, nonviolence and the like. The church believes that it is possible to prevent bloodshed when there is a crisis.

Let me give you two of my own experiences in peacemaking where there were conflicts. The first conflict was between Christians and Muslims in Chinene in 1979. The village of Chinene is not far from Favva and Ngoshe. It is about nine kilometers from Gavva, where I was living at that time, and about one kilometer from Amuda, situated in Gwoza East. Gwoza is one of the jurisdictions of Borno State.

On April 28, 1979, a church building that the Ekklesiyar Yan'uwa a Nigeria (EYN) had constructed was destroyed by some Muslims. The watchman on duty escaped and went to some Christian brothers to inform them what had happened. Actually the Muslims were complaining that Christians always built churches outside the town, but this church was built in the center of town. So on April 29 the news spread quickly to Gavva, Amuda, Ngoshe, Barawa, Arboko, Atagara, Agapalawa, Bokko, Jibirili, Chikide, and other villages. About two thousand Christian men gathered at Amuda, very close to Chinene. The purpose of the gathering was to go to war to revenge the destruction of the Chinene church. Christians were furious because so many such incidents had happened to them, but nothing had been done.

During the meeting I asked them a question, "What will happen after we go to war? Probably one person will be killed among us and maybe one among the Muslims. How can we compare the two lives with the building? The building was not yet under roof. Even if it were under roof, which would be of more value, the lives we might lose or the building?" The majority said that the lives we were going to lose would be of more value.

So one of the ministers quickly intervened by saying, "Let's take the matter to court instead of going to war." The majority supported the idea of going to court, except for one person who became very angry and left the meeting saying, "I knew that since Filibus was here, nothing would work." A few weeks after the matter was taken to court, the man who started hitting the building with a shovel became deranged. Another man who had organized the destruction died suddenly. People were amazed and afraid. Many people in Chinene became Christians that year. They built another church to replace the one that was destroyed. A Christian man, Mr. Yusufu Wariga, is now the head of the village of Chinene. Reverend Ibrahim D. Ashifa is the village head of Amuda. He supported me during the meeting at Amuda in making the decision not to go to fight the Chinene Muslims. He supported me in withdrawing the plan for war.

The second conflict occurred in October 1980. We went to Bokko to show films about the life of our Lord Jesus Christ. When it came to the point where Jesus was on the cross, a Muslim man said, "You Christian are liars. Jesus didn't die on the cross. It was somebody else."

Our evangelist who was working in the village of Bokko became angry. "Why do you call us liars?" The Muslim man repeated, "You are liars [shege]." The Muslim man and the evangelist started pouring out abusive words. They were neighbors. Each one of them ran to his house to get weapons. I quickly sent some young Christian brothers to go and lock the door of the evangelist so that he couldn't come out of the house with his weapons.

Already the Muslim man was outside with his bow and arrows waiting for the evangelist to come outside so he could shoot him. By that time I had stopped the program; I begged the Muslim man to be patient and go back into his house. After the program I took the evangelist to another place and later transferred him to a different village.

In the same village of Bokko in 1981, a pastor was teaching Christian Religious Knowledge (CRK) in the primary school. When I went to visit the school, I met the Christian children outside the classroom under a tree. The CRK teacher told me that there was an empty classroom inside, but the headmaster said that the Christian pupils should be taught outside. The headmaster claimed that he didn't say this, but the pastor insisted that he did. They started beating each other in front of me. I had to step between them. I quickly took the CRK teacher away, then came back the following day to talk to the headmaster. We agreed that he should find another CRK teacher.

This shows the current position of the Church of the Brethren in Nigeria. We hate war, and many Nigerian Brothers and sisters will definitely refuse go to war or kill. The Church of the Brethren in Nigeria, especially in Adamawa and Borno states where the majority of EYN members live, are well known for their concern for peace through reconciliation. There have been many religious clashes, but EYN members do not retaliate. EYN is showing its commitment to peace between other churches and with the government. EYN has confronted the government many times about issues related to peace and justice. The church is more aware of itself now as a peace church than ever before. In 2004 the theme of our annual conference on March 31 to April 3 was "The Role of EYN in Peacemaking."

These efforts are not because we are pacifists, but because we have learned to love our neighbors as ourselves. It will take time for the church to recognize pacifism, but some are now moving in that direction. The main concern of the early missionaries was the gospel of reconciliation as the main path to peace among brothers and sisters in Christ. The main biblical texts cited were Matthew, chapter 18; John 13; 1 Corinthians 13; and Matthew, chapter 5 through chapter 7. Through biblical teaching and practical life witness, the EYN church has come to know peace as the source of life. We have come to recognize reconciliation as the source of peace. We are peacemakers without claiming to be pacifists.

This was manifested in my life when I was the chairman of the Christian Association of Nigeria (CAN), Borno State branch, 1998 to 2002. If it were not for my background as a member of the Church of the Brethren in Nigeria, there might have been a religious crisis when Sharia law was introduced into the Borno State in 1999 and 2000. Christians were ready to take sides and go to war. But because I have learned about the value of life, I resisted any violence and called for nonviolent resistance.

I am glad for EYN's connection with the Church of the Brethren, the Society of Friends, and the Mennonite Central Committee, all of whom are well known for their love for peace, for humankind, and for all creation. I am sure that EYN will learn from these peace churches through our visits, prayers, and conversations. Our foundation is in a Christianity which is peace itself. Let us go forth to teach, preach, and practice the gospel of love and reconciliation to the whole world.

> Peace I leave with you. My own peace I now bequeath to you. Not as the world giveth do I give to you. Do not let your hearts be troubled; neither let them be afraid. Stop allowing yourselves to be agitated and disturbed. Do not permit yourselves to be fearful and intimidated and cowardly and unsettled. (John 14:27, Amplified Bible)

A major source for the wording and subject matter of this chapter is "Reconciliation or Pacifism? The Nigerian Experience," by Patrick K. Bugu, in Seeking Cultures of Peace: A Peace Church Conversation, *ed. Fernando Enns, Scott Holland, and Ann Riggs; Cascadia, World Council of Churches, and Herald Press, 2004, ch 8, 124-131; copyright © 2004, Cascadia Publishing House, and used by permission.*

7

WHO ARE WE?

Fernando Enns (Germany)

WHO ARE WE? WE ARE MEMBERS OF THE Historic Peace Churches: Church of the Brethren, Friends, Mennonites, Brethren in Christ. The roots of these traditions go a long way back. Some of our roots reach to the Anabaptist movement in the sixteenth century in Europe. Among these Anabaptists were those who criticized the political powers as well as the ruling church. When it became clear that they would not be able to reform the church, they decided to form an alternative, as did many other churches that emerged from the Reformation.

What caused the Anabaptists to criticize the mainstream church so severely? First of all, the Anabaptists developed a vision of a visible church, a community of believers that would strive to live according to the teachings and example of Jesus. Their vision was of a church that not only confessed and believed in Jesus Christ as the Son of God, through whom the love of God to all creation was revealed, but a church that actually lived as if with Jesus the kingdom of God had already come into a fallen, unjust, and violent world. They were convinced that the church was called to be a sign of hope in itself, a "city on a hill," the "salt of the earth."

Central to the Anabaptist vision of the church was becoming a people of peace. Thus nonviolence became one of the regulative principles for their ecclesiology, based on the cross, where God had shown that his nonviolence to creation rejected the use of violence even when God's own self was threatened on the cross. Jesus suffered death to reveal the hopelessness of the way of violence and to prove the truth that love and nonviolence will overcome all evil, even death, in the end.

The Historic Peace Churches have accepted this core interpretation of the cross as our heritage. Consequently we have taken seriously the teachings of the gospel not only to love the neighbor but to love the enemy; not only to go one mile but to go the second mile; not only to be against violence but to seek healing wherever relationships have been violated or broken. This we believe to be the core mission of the church. The church will only be faithful when it seeks nonviolent ways of conflict resolution, when it does not accept violence as a way for true believers. Evil will be overcome by good, as Romans 12 states.

A second answer to our question of who we are is that we are Christians in communion with other Christians. The Historic Peace Churches have shared their convictions with other believers. And the ecumenical movement of the twentieth century provided a space for the Historic Peace Churches to witness and to explain their beliefs to the other churches after the mainline churches had for centuries oppressed and discriminated against them.

In this process we have come to understand that the pacifist tradition and emphasis on a theologically grounded ethics of nonviolence and an active involvement for peacebuilding is not understood by other traditions in the same way as we do. Nevertheless, the other churches have asked us again and again to stay committed to the ecumenical family and have welcomed us in the ecumenical community of churches. Accordingly, many in the Historic Peace Churches have committed themselves to this ecumenical movement, because being ecumenical is part of the peace witness of every church.

Within the ecumenical movement, we have been able to initiate a new process to open a wide ecumenical space that will truly help us, together with others, to develop many creative nonviolent alternatives to conflict. The Decade to Overcome Violence, initiated by the World Council of Churches, began in 2001 and will last until 2010. The subtitle of the decade is Churches Seeking Reconciliation and Peace. This decade is in itself a sign of faithfulness, since Christians of all traditions are accepting the challenge and are committing themselves to the efforts of overcoming violence. We are on our way to identifying sustainable ways for peacebuilding, for reconciliation based on just relationships.

But to be clear, this decade is not only a challenge to the other traditions. It is as well a challenge to the Historic Peace Churches, because we ourselves are as puzzled by the ambiguities of violence as our brothers and sisters of other traditions. We are struggling with injustice, economic imbalance, cruelty, and war, and very often we do not know the answers. We want peace, but how do we reach it? We want to protect the defenseless, but how can we achieve it? We want reconciliation, but what are the steps to forgiveness and healing?

Who are we really? We are people of faith—Christians, Historic Peace Churches in the ecumenical family. Who are we in Africa, this continent where violence often speaks such a visible language? Who are we, struggling, searching, asking and praying, fighting for peace? This decade is a wonderful opportunity to discern together, to strengthen each other, to share the unanswered questions and challenges. Above all, it is an opportunity to celebrate God's never ending mercy, God's sustaining grace and forgiveness to all our failures, God's justification despite all our weaknesses. God will make us what we are called to be, a people of peace. May God guide our discerning, and may God grant us wisdom and courage to be honest about our own weaknesses and complicity in violence, and make us strong in our efforts to overcome violence throughout Africa and around the world.

Part III

THE STORIES OF VIOLENCE IN ITS MANY FORMS

Stories and personal narratives about the violence, genocide, warfare, rape, AIDS/HIV, corruption, poverty, and oppression that continue to take place in Africa

8

THREATS TO PEACE

Ahmed Haile (Kenya)

I WOULD LIKE TO ADDRESS THREE ISSUES that I believe are threats to peace. The first issue is the threat to peace that comes by doing nothing about violence and ethnic conflict. The second issue is ethnicity. And the third issue is terrorism and counter-terrorism.

To this end I want to tell a Somali fable. Once upon a time two men journeyed to a foreign country. One was a brave fighter well-known by all Somalis. The other was a famous coward. These two men continued to journey until they reached a place full of danger. The brave man turned to the coward and said to him, "We have come to a dangerous place, and we must work together. Otherwise we are going to die. Take the front and protect us from the danger that we must face from the front. Or take the back and defend us from the danger from the back."

He was a coward. What would you expect from him? If he went in front, he feared that the animals would jump on him. If he went to the back, he also feared that the animals would jump on him. He looked at the brave man and said, "Many people say that I am a coward. We will walk side by side." The man decided that he would not lead and he would not be led. The choice was to continue as they were.

This fable is appropriate to all of us familiar with the peace churches. We have come to a dangerous place. The world is not a peaceful place. Either we lead or we can push from the back. I know

Mennonite Central Committee and the peace churches have a Washington office and they are pushing from the back. But also we can go to the front. The coward refused to take the front or the back because for him both the front and the back threatened violence and death. The moral of the story is that the coward chose a third option: doing nothing.

I would like us to look at what the Historic Peace Churches stand for. What is this idea of peace? What is the meaning of peace? A concept is an idea, usually expressed in a sentence or a phrase, by which we think, criticize, argue, explain, or analyze. Shalom as a concept is an idea to which we all hold. The word comes from Hebrew and is one all Africans understand. No African comes to your home unless he says "Shalom" to you. First he will say "Shalom," then he will keep talking. Or he will say "but," then he will tell you that the cows are sick, the farm crops are not growing, and the children are sick. That tells you that shalom is the well-being of the whole community, not just of the individual or family. It is about wholeness, the intactness of the whole community. Peace also has a meaning that comes from the Greek. In the Bible it refers to linkage or order. As Africans, we are linked together in peace. The gospel is a gospel of peace, a gospel that reconciles.

So we conclude that shalom has three meanings. The first is relationship. The African community has a problem in that in many cases relationships are not working. People will tell you, "There is no shalom because people are fighting." People have a problem. Actually we find that our peace is threatened by all the broken relationships around us.

Second, shalom is restorative. The African way of understanding is mending relationships. I've never seen any African culture in which if one person kills another, the clan and the families do not come together to mend the relationships. Africans don't believe in an eye for an eye. My culture doesn't believe violence is a way of restoring relationships. Retributive justice is not found in most African cultures.

The third meaning of shalom is a moral and ethical one. If people in a community are lying to each other, then there will be no shalom. In Africa when people talk about politics, they will say that what you hear about politics is a deception. In Africa, cheating takes away shalom. Such immorality is a threat to peace.

Islam is another word for shalom. The words *Salam, Islam, Muslim, Jerusalem, Salem,* and *Solomon* are all derived from the word for peace. That word has three consonants: *s*, *l*, and *m*. It is the same word in Arabic as in Hebrew. However, achieving peace in certain ways can also be a threat to peace. The Romans imposed peace by conquest, by bringing the barbarians under control. There was a dichotomy between the barbarian and the Pax Romana. Islam believes the same, and the dichotomy is between the house of Islam and the house of war.

This is also what we usually hear from the West, which all of us are imitating. I tell my students that if Michael Jackson sings a certain way or moves a certain way, all African youth will do the same. We are imitating something that is not ours. A prominent American military leader is reported to have said that he was running out of demons. This tells you that you have to have a scapegoat to make peace. You have to have a problem with someone else so that you can unite. This happens with Africans too. When we have a family dysfunction, we try to create some problem outside ourselves, then we use the tribal and clan system as a solution. The same idea has come from U.S. President George W. Bush. He has talked of the "axis of evil" that includes Syria, Iraq, and Iran. Here we have a problem, a threat to peace. Wars created by politics and armaments are a threat to peace.

Let me come to ethnicity, also a threat to peace. This is a particularly African issue. We Africans have a problem. In the church we have a problem. We can talk about other things, but in the church basically we are divided into tribes, clans, and families. We all come together as a peace church, but when we go home, we are different. In my culture we say that in the daytime we are one thing, but at night time we become another. To put it differently, in the daytime we are family, but at night are divided into our mothers' families. You remember that African polygamists have a traditional practice. In the daytime we will all defend each other, but at night time we go to our mother's home because our father has many wives. So in the nighttime we are divided and in the day time we are together. This is a problem that we are facing.

One form of violence is the hatred many ethnic and religious groups have for each other. We can talk about hate in Bosnia, Serbia, and Chechnya, but it is also here. It is in Kenya, Nigeria, Somalia, Ethiopia, Zambia, and Zimbabwe. We know that it is in Rwanda and Burundi. In the daytime we are all Rwandans or Burundians. We will talk about well-being to each other as we greet each other, but in the night-time there is no well-being. There is no peace.

Now let me move into this whole idea of terrorism and counter-terrorism, for they are also threats to peace. They perpetuate violence. We all remember what happened on September 11. As I came from the school, I saw the replay of the second plane hitting the Twin Towers. The image of the Twin Towers and everybody who was hurt remains with us. Yet the threat could have been solved differently. It has become a problem, particularly for me, every time I travel. I have to take off my shoes, and because of my missing leg I am not able to tie and untie my shoe laces.

In Africa we say that when two elephants fight, it is the grass that suffers. Someone has put it in a little more interesting way. When two elephants are making love, the grass also suffers. When the people of the West hate one another, it is still Africa that suffers. Who is threatened? Where are these wars fought? What is our proper response to the threat to peace? Are the terrorists targeting only the Americans? The answer is simple. Terrorists are not only a threat to the U.S.—but also a threat to all nations. We are all in the same boat.

Again, here is an area in which the churches have a job, particularly the peace churches. How do we deal with terrorism? All are interested in this problem, whether they are theologians, political scientists, psychologists, or sociologists. However, the word *terror* means many things to many people. A bomb can hit your home when you are on a plane doing your part as a member of a peace church. It can happen to anyone.

The concept of threat is the determination to use punishment, injury, and death to produce tension. The U.S. military defines terrorism as the unlawful use of threat, force, and violence against individuals and property to coerce or intimidate a government or society. Often the goal is to obtain a political, religious, or ideological objective. Another political scientist defines terrorism as the use of violence for intimidation, coercion, or instilling fear to obtain goals that are political, religious, or ideological in nature. Anyone who uses violence in this way and for these goals becomes a terrorist.

This is the threat to peace in which we find ourselves. But who suffers? The people who suffer are innocent non-combatants, children, mothers, and fathers who have become the target of violence. What do we mean by the threat to peace then? Who is threatened? What is the proper response in this area then? We can ask this question again and again.

I would like to conclude in this way: We have set for ourselves three areas of concern. One is to preach the gospel of peace to all nations, which includes loving your enemy. Another area comes to us as individuals. You might call it ethnic hatred. It can be in the church as when a bishop turns on his congregation. And the third area that I have discussed is the idea of terrorism. In our day terrorism is something we all live with. We in the church, especially in the Historic Peace Churches, need to articulate how we will deal with it. A decade of overcoming violence is also a decade of overcoming terrorism.

PRAYER
SALAMATU JOEL BILLI (NIGERIA)

Our Father, we come before you with hearts full of gratitude. Father, we thank you that you have awakened our minds to the fact that we are ambassadors of peace. We know that we are not better than anyone else, but that it is through your grace that we are here. We thank you for the salvation you have given us. We thank you, Lord, for so many things.

Father, we want to remember those who have been traumatized. You know each and every one of them. We pray that you will heal them in your special way. Our Lord and our God, we want to thank you for the stories from Rwanda and Burundi and other places where you have enabled Christians to show your light. We pray that you will fill them with your love that has no boundary, that you will continue to show your love to people, and that they will have forgiving hearts. That, Lord, where there are wounds, you will heal.

Our Lord and our God, we pray for those who have ethnic problems. Lord, may you teach Christians that we should know first and foremost that we are your children, and then we are members of our tribes.

Father, may you be able to touch the hearts of Christians, especially these peace churches, that Lord we will work up to our responsibilities and never be tired but be willing to work for you, to bring peace wherever we find ourselves.

Father, we thank you because we know that you are going to be with us, you are going to give us more power, you are going to enable us, Lord, to work for the cause of peace everywhere we find ourselves. For we pray in Jesus name. Amen.

9

OBSTACLES TO PEACE IN AFRICA

Abraham Wuta Tizhe (Nigeria)

LET US LOOK AT THE ISSUES OF PEACE IN AFRICA under the following three topics: (1), conflicts and wars in Africa; (2) International agents of peace; and (3) obstacles to peace in Africa.

CONFLICTS AND WARS IN AFRICA

With a great land mass of 11,680,000 square miles, Africa is the second largest continent on earth. It has a population estimated to be 900,000,000 (*National Geographic*, August 2005). The continent has a vast desert which covers 3,300,000 square miles, dense tropical forests, and rivers difficult to navigate. The Nile River is the longest river in the world and very useful for irrigation. With an area of 26,828 square miles, Lake Victoria is the second-largest fresh-water lake in the world and is a good resource for fishing and irrigation. Africa is the home of many kinds of animals, both domesticated and wild. Dr. Louis S. B. Leakey's discovery in Africa of the oldest known human skull, estimated to be 2,000,000 years old, means that it is possible all the human race came from this continent.

Despite all these resources, Africa is the least developed continent on our planet in terms of industry and transportation systems. It was carved into colonies during the scramble for control by the European powers of Belgium, Germany, Great Britain, France, Italy, Portugal, and Spain. The continent remained under colonial rule until the mid-twentieth century, following which some new nations have emerged. However, the continent has experienced many internal problems since independence, especially regarding how to achieve governments that are economically stable, productive, and efficient.

Since countries earlier under colonial control are relatively peaceful today, why are there so many conflicts and wars in Africa? Have African countries not been emulating their former colonial masters' good systems of government? Yes, some colonial powers generated good models of government. However, a failing of these colonial governments was concentration on exporting resources rather than helping Africans develop reliable sources of food and water. Even today Africa suffers constant hunger, conflict, and war. There is still war in Sudan, especially involving the Jinjaweed militia in the Darfur region. There is war in Liberia, Ivory Coast, and Equatorial Guinea. There is war within Rwanda and Burundi and between Ethiopia and Eritrea. Religious and political conflicts in Nigeria have resulted in many killings and great loss of property. There are conflicts in Zimbabwe. In the Democratic Republic of Congo (DCR) there is an ongoing struggle for power and many lives have been lost.

INTERNATIONAL AGENTS OF PEACE

While there have been many conflicts and wars in Africa, there also have been movements to reduce conflict. The Organization for African Unity was an agency we hoped would bring peace to a conflicted Africa. How many conflicts or wars it has settled is not yet clear. Recently it has changed its name to the African Union and now has sent troops to the region of Darfur for peacekeeping. The Economic Community of West African States (ECOWAS) is also an organization seeking to promote peace in the West African region, but nevertheless war has been going on in Sierra Leone. Agents of peace like the Permanent Court of International Justice sought to bring a lasting peace to the conflicts and wars in Africa.

The United Nations' Codification of International Law intended to stop the conflicts and wars in Africa, but to no avail. The United Nations was established for settling the problems of conflicts and wars going on around the world, especially in Africa, which has been without peace for decades. The agencies for peace like The World Health Organization (WHO), The New Partnership for Africa's Development (NEPAD), the United Nations (UN), Food and Agriculture Organization (FAO), and The World Trade Organization (WTO), as well as military observers in Congo and Sudan have sought to bring lasting solutions to the conflicts and wars in Africa.

From a Christian point of view, it is a sad fact that international law has made warfare legal, because such law respects what has become an accepted practice of nation-states. Warfare is described by the UN as "armed conflict" rather than "war." So what can the world at large do to make peace among the African states? When will Africa stop being a testing ground for the new weapons of the developed nations? When will the above-mentioned organizations achieve their peacemaking objectives?

OBSTACLES TO PEACE IN AFRICA

The Africans themselves cannot bring about peace due to the following obstacles. Differences of opinion have led some leaders into conflicts and subsequently wars that resulted in many people losing their lives for their own beliefs and attitudes. Although religious conflicts have not led to wars in Africa like those in Europe during the Reformation era, such conflicts are a serious threat to peace in Africa. Cultural differences that breed suspicion and misunderstanding can easily lead to conflicts and wars. Even differing ideologies between tribes can lead to conflict.

Despite these problems, something must be done for peace in Africa. This requires attending to economic conditions. The world is divided into "have" and "have-not" states. Countries in the developed world need to see beyond their own horizons and help Africa if peace is to be restored. In most cases conflicts and wars in Africa are a result of hunger, poor health conditions, poverty, and economic struggles. Acquisition of natural resources generates tension and war, and unless we do something in this regard, more African nations will engage in conflict. The Bakassi Peninsula between Nigeria and Cameroon is an example. Many lives have been lost there!

Continuation of the arms race among the developed nations is surely a threat to Africa. Unless something is done to stop arms sales, it will be hard to achieve peace in Africa's affected regions. The rise of nationalism among people in Africa is another factor hampering the achievement of peace in Africa. The Hutus and the Tutsi represent one instance. To be effective, the people of peace must do something to address these economic, political, social, and religious threats to peace.

WHERE WAS THE CHURCH?
PATSON NETHA (ZIMBABWE)

We are in a decade to overcome violence, and what a challenge that is for us as Christians. I belong to a very interesting country, a very controversial one, a very nice one too, called Zimbabwe. When our president decided the troops would go to Congo, there was no consultation with Parliament at all. The legislators knew nothing. As a church, we went into the place where they were, and we said to them,"How can you do this?"

They looked back at us and they said, "It is according to a protocol already decided, one of the protocols for security; and therefore we are supposed to defend any of our countries, any of our legitimate governments that are being attacked."

And I screamed, "Where was I, as a church? Where were we, as a church, when these protocols were being formed? We never gave input into them."

Where are we, as the church? Are we putting our influence into what those in power are deciding, into what they are doing? Do we have a voice in what's happening? If we are going to be involved in the issues of peace, we need to get our voice into these protocols from their onset. In order for morality to be included in them and in order for a Christian basis and a theological understanding to be considered in them, we need to be people who are involved in working at advocacy. We cannot afford anymore not to be involved in these things. It is no longer a luxury. It is a necessity. It is no longer something we can be far from. We have to be close to the decision-makers in order for us, as a church, to be able to give our input to them. That is the only way we can stop being reactive and start becoming proactive.

For us to have peace in Africa, we have got to be involved in bodies such as the African Union, so that we can speak to the powers that be, so that we can walk in the corridors of power, bringing both the message of the gospel into these places, and at the same time uplifting our call to peace.

10

POST-INDEPENDENCE VIOLENCE IN ZIMBABWE

Albert Ndlovu (Zimbabwe)

I AM A MEMBER OF THE BRETHREN IN CHRIST CHURCH in Zimbabwe and pastor a church there. I belong to the Peace and Justice Committee of our conference, which we started at the Mennonite World Conference in 2003. I am also a member of the group Grace to Heal, a peace and justice organization. I want to present what happened in Zimbabwe after independence. Much of what I will say is contained in a book prepared by the Board of Justice and Peace of the Catholic Church in Zimbabwe. This is a very personal story to me, since I am telling this story not only as someone who was observing what was happening but also as a victim.

Zimbabwe, like many independent states the world over, waged a fierce battle to free itself from colonial rule; in our case this took fifteen years. The black majority had suffered from colonial rule for almost ninety years. The struggle for independence saw a split within a political party then known as the Zimbabwe African Peoples Union—ZAPU—leading to the formation of a second party, the Zimbabwe African Naional Union—ZANU. The two parties' members were drawn primarily from two tribes, the Ndebele and Shona respectively. The two parties had armed factions, ZIPRA and ZANLA, and many casualties occurred as the parties and their armed affiliates jostled for power.

Just before independence, Robert Mugabe emerged as the leader of ZANU while Joshua Nkomo was the leader of ZAPU. This was after reconciliation efforts between the two parties were disrupted by the ZANU group through mysterious accidents and deaths among those who supported the initiative by Joshua Nkomo to have a united patriotic front. One of the victims was ZANLA High Command leader Josiah Tongogara.

At the celebration of Zimbabwe's independence on April 18, 1980, Robert Mugabe assumed the national presidency and spoke about the need for forgiveness and reconciliation. Unfortunately, these were promises on which he would not deliver. In July a state of emergency that had been in place since 1965 was renewed, then and every six months after that until 1990. Soon President Mugabe signed an agreement with the North Koreans to train and arm a brigade of the Zimbabwe defense forces.

IN 1981

There were outbreaks of violence between the two liberation armies, and the government appointed a commission to inquire into the disturbances. A respected judge, the late Enock Dumbutshena, led the investigation team. The findings still have not been made public, since the report would have pointed to government responsibility for the violence. South Africa stepped up sabotage activities with ease as some of their spies joined Zimbabwe's intelligence and military forces. In August 1981, the North Korean instructors arrived to begin training the "Fifth Brigade" that was to be used to "combat the dissidents."

The sad part of this situation was that there were genuine grievances that could have been addressed. South African agents sabotaged the ZANU headquarters, killing seven and injuring 124. The insecurity in the country gave an opportunity for both South Africa and ZANU to blame the unrest on the opposition.

IN 1982

Arms caches were "discovered" in Matebeleland, and the government responded by arresting the opposition ZAPU commanders and expelling ZAPU leaders from the cabinet. Ex-ZIPRA cadres defected in large numbers from the integrated army and banditry activities increased. An abortive attack on Mugabe's residence was linked to the opposition. South African agents sabotaged the air base, destroying thirteen military planes.

All these disturbances led to the imposition of a curfew, detentions, and weapon searches in Bulawayo, the capital city of Matebeleland. The curfew engulfed the whole of Matebeleland after six foreign tourists were kidnapped. People in rural Matebeleland formed many armed groups and the detention of ex-ZIPRA cadres and ZAPU supporters continued. There was much concern for the innocent within the society as ruthless means were exercised to force confessions. This prompted churches, especially the Catholics, to prepare reports showing that innocent people were suffering and calling on the government to maintain the rule of law. However, this appeal fell on deaf ears.

IN 1983-84

The Fifth Brigade completed its training and was ready for deployment in Matebeleland. This was the period during which the worst state-orchestrated violence in memory was to follow. The Fifth Brigade was deployed in Matebeleland and immediately began raping, maiming, beating, and burning villagers. There was restricted movement, and the suffering of the communities was worse than has ever been told. The well-calculated restrictions of movement left even the churches crippled. These atrocities worsened day by day, as all possible forms of torture were exercised. Pregnant women had their bellies ripped open so state agents could see "dissidents" in the womb.

Ndebele-speaking people were generally ZAPU supporters and the Shona majority ZANU. This gave an excuse for the state agents to set in motion an ethnic cleansing spree, claiming all the villagers of Matebeleland were dissidents and collaborators. The atrocities spread to the whole of Matebeleland and the Midlands province, seeming to be a well-calculated move to whip the nation into a one-party state without declaring it. Zimbabwe was due to hold its second general election in 1985. Pre-election violence raged on as youth brigades and ZANU supporters pounced on the people in Matebeleland. The suffering that the people of these regions went through is sad to ponder and it is even sadder that for many people these events remain completely unknown.

In bizarre madness the perpetrators would beat their victims to a pulp in public, make them dig their graves, then force them into the graves, where they were piled on each other and shot. Whether the victims were dead or not, the public witnesses of these killings would be forced to cover the bodies with soil while they continued singing ZANU songs. Some were left to the dogs and other scavengers. Some disappeared as they were thrown into mine shafts. Mourning, an integral part of facilitating the healing related to the loss of loved ones, was not allowed. After numerous condemnations of the killings by the churches, a commission of inquiry was set up and gathered evidence of army atrocities, raising hopes of a solution. But its findings remain unknown twenty years later.

IN 1987

The outcome of the presidential election was a forgone conclusion, but the suffering people of Matebeleland continued to vote for the opposition, which they have continued to do since then. Violence continued for a long time after the election. Government intelligence agents continued to harass and kill ZAPU supporters and many innocent civilians were detained. Five of our church members in Bulawayo were picked up from a Sunday morning church service, and one disappeared completely. At the same time, opposition leader Joshua Nkomo and President Robert Mugabe were discussing a unity agreement that brought an end to the darkest moment of our independence era. Some 15,000 and 20,000 innocent people had been killed in this terrible time of violence.

After the unity agreement went into force, amnesty for all the dissidents was announced, and more than a hundred of them surrendered. Amnesty was later extended to all members of the army who committed atrocities before the Unity Accord. Any talk of the traumatized victims attracts the anger of the president and his supporters, who say this was a moment of madness and old wounds should be left alone so they can be "healed naturally." For the victims, those were the worst moments in their lives, and the absence of any government apologies only makes the situation worse. The shallow unmarked graves, the scars, and the children from rape are among the depressing reminders that still haunt them.

IN 2000

The elections of 1990 and 1995 were peaceful, but an opposition movement arose in 1999. During the 2000 elections there was a new outbreak of violence, this time around the whole country. Torture chambers came back. and disappearances became the norm. The famous "land to the people" chorus was sung everywhere. Many land owners, the majority of whom were white, lost their land.

An opposition member was picked up from his house by some men said to be supporting the ruling party—and that man was not seen again. Those who kidnapped this man bragged about it for quite a long time. Six men were arrested for being involved in this kidnapping, including a member of parliament, but the courts are saying that the opposition was not responsible.

CURRENTLY

There are many sad things about the situation in Zimbabwe today. With respect to the cry for "land to the people," it is sad to note that some of those who got the land are losing that land now to the political right. When you go to Zimbabwe, you may think there is peace, but what about the estimated 3.5 million from Zimbabwe who are in the Diaspora? And what about the million in the United Kingdom and the several hundred thousand in Canada? And the value of our currency has declined alarmingly. A year ago with $1 U.S. you would get $2,500 of our money. Now it would take $6,500 Zimbabwe dollars to buy $1 U.S. We are all millionaires. But this is a cruel joke. In fact, we are poor millionaires.

Currently our government has a "National Youth Service." The common name for them is "Green Bombers." Unfortunately, the young people are not actually being deployed into national service; they are only being "trained." They are being given uniforms, so they seem to have some authority in the community, and they feel they are important. Who are the Green Bombers? They are the ones now serving as the militia for the government under the pretext of doing national service. And what do they do when they get into the camps? Basically they are taught how to kill, to torture, and how to inflict a great deal of pain. The camps become a free-for-all. Boys and girls sleep in the same place. Girls are raped all through the night. It is pathetic. Most of the people that come out of those camps test HIV-positive. We have had children born in these camps who are HIV-positive as well.

I know this is a very sad story, but I can only report what has been happening in the recent past and is continuing to happen. We in Zimbabwe are much in need of your prayer and your understanding.

11
_____

LOOTING IN THE CONGO

Cathy Mputu (Congo)

AS WE CONSIDER THE THREATS TO PEACE IN AFRICA, I have chosen to describe a painful event that took place in the Congo, a very sad case of widespread looting. In the Democratic Republic of Congo, one of the Great Lakes countries, we have experienced difficulties and civil war almost the entire time since 1960, when we were given our independence. In the early years, the turmoil allowed Colonel Joseph Mobutu to seize power in a coup d' etat. The persistence of this cycle of violence provided an excuse for the establishment of a dictatorial and militaristic regime based on Mobutu's party, the MPR. This dictatorial system pushed the country into a kind of political conflict that became even more chaotic in the 1990s.

In 1991 the negative events began with the opening of the sessions of the Conference on National Sovereignty. For the Zairean people at that time (Zaire was the name President Mobutu gave the country to signal a new emphasis on African-ness), this conference was a long-awaited lifeboat, our only hope to uproot the tyrant and lead our county out of the abyss.

Unfortunately the hope that the Zairean people had for this conference went up in smoke and left our people with distrust and anger. The government's elite paratroopers, who had not received their back pay, began pillaging the stores, warehouses, service stations, administrative offices, and homes of the wealthy in Kinshasha, the capital city. The troops continued the looting day and night for two days. It began to appear that the looting would not be stopped, as it spread from the military personnel to the ordinary citizens.

While this was underway, we who lived in Kinshasha went to our gates to watch the spectacle. We saw a parade of people—men, women, children—carrying huge cardboard boxes of stolen merchandise and pushing shopping carts filled with food, appliances, and everything imaginable. They all hurried to their homes as though they had received an unbelievable supply of Christmas gifts. Those who originally refrained from participating soon jumped into the fray, not wanting to miss their chance to escape from poverty. People cheered the looters as they came back for more. Some of the looters even began offering their bounty for sale.

Unfortunately, many Christians joined in this frenzy of looting in Kinshasha. In subsequent prayer meetings and worship services, many of these Christian looters testified to God's goodness in providing for them. As the Reverend Doctor Lumeya said, "We have to wonder what is wrong if committed Christians can jump into the action and rejoice with the looters."

This sad event cost the businesses loss of goods worth some 700 million in U.S. dollars, and about 75,000 workers lost their jobs when these businesses were closed. The middle class in Kinshasha is still suffering today because of these losses and because of the many other causes of political and economic chaos.

During the time of the looting, a second threat to peace was developing. President Mobutu did everything he could to hinder the efforts of the political leaders to establish a legitimate civilian government. He refused to acknowledge the legitimacy of Prime Minister Etienne Tshisekedi. Instead, Mobutu turned his troops loose on the helpless population, bringing panic and disorder to Kinshasha. This time many private homes as well as shops and offices were looted. After eight in the evening, the streets were totally deserted. People hid their electrical appliances and other valuables here and there, turned off all their lights, and remained silent so as not to attract the soldiers' attention.

Despite these efforts, many homes were looted. There was rape, torture, even massacre. The people of Kinshasha have never fully recovered from this horrible series of lootings. Even today, hospitals are lacking in supplies, equipment, and medicine. The work ethic has been undermined by the memory of getting so many things of value from the looting. Basic things like public transportation are no longer available. What a sad part of our national history this is.

12

WARFARE
IN SOUTH KIVU

Ramazani Kakozi (Congo)

I WANT TO FOCUS ON EVENTS IN BUKAVU that have so shaken the town. Bukavu is the capital of South Kivu province, one of eleven provinces in the Democratic Republic of Congo (DRC). To fully understand the crisis in Bukavu and its consequences, we should briefly recall details that have marked the history of Congo since its independence, especially in South Kivu. Part of the eastern edge of South Kivu is formed by Lake Tanganyika; other parts of the border are shared with Rwanda, Burundi, Uganda, and Tanzania. This is important because these countries have been involved in the events we are considering.

Since its independence on June 30, 1960, the Democratic Republic of the Congo has frequently known war. All of these wars, with the exception of the civil wars in 1960-61, had their beginnings in South Kivu. I will discuss only four.

First, the Mulelist rebellion started in Lemera in 1964. The Mulelists, named after their leader Pierre Mulele, were not from South Kivu. They were from Bandu province but came to South Kivu to make war.

Second, the revolt of the mercenaries commanded by Jean Schramme targeted the town of Bukavu in 1967.

Third, in 1996 the so-called war of liberation led by the late President Laurent-Désiré Kabila and his Alliance of Democratic Forces for the Liberation of Congo/Zaire (AFDL) started in Lemera.

Fourth, in 1998 the so-called war of rectification, led by the Rally for Congolese Democracy (Rassemblement Congolais pour la Démocratie—RCD) and its Rwandan allies, also started in South Kivu, at Uvira and Bukavu.

As you can see from this outline, the province of South Kivu has been something of a time bomb, threatening peace in Congo. Unless national and international authorities come up with viable solutions to the issues in this province, the Great Lakes region will once again erupt in violence. If there is no peace in South Kivu, there will be none in Rwanda or Burundi either. I am sure the most knowledgeable international leaders are well aware of this.

To return to the war of 1998, this war has been considered by some to be the first African world war. Several countries were involved. On the one side were countries like Rwanda, Burundi, and Uganda, all supporting the rebels. On the other side were Angola, Chad, and Zimbabwe, who sided with the Kinshasa government. We should also note that the U.S. and United Kingdom in one way or another supported the first faction, while France and other European countries aided the second faction. This war had two dimensions: the external dimension, which consisted of the involvement of these six countries, and the internal dimension, concerning which even Congolese authorities say relatively little.

I want to discuss the internal dimension of the conflict in 1998, concentrating on South Kivu. Our province has serious intertribal conflict, but this is something people don't talk about very often. The problem can be narrowed down to the identity of the Bamyamulenge group. While it might seem that the problem of intertribal rivalry might easily be resolved, the problem of the Bamyamulenge is so difficult that if it is not resolved, likely there will be another war. The Congolese are divided over whether or not the Bamyamulenge are foreigners, that is Rwandans, instead of Congolese. Those who consider them to be foreigners point out that when war broke out in Uganda, the Bamyamulenge sent their children to join the rebel army in Uganda, because the Uganda government had sided with Rwanda. When war broke out in Rwanda in 1994, the Bamyamulenge also sent their children to do military service there.

In 1996 when the war in Congo with Laurent Desire Kabila began, Kabila had no soldiers. Those who joined his rebellion were largely Bamyamulenge, which is why this war is sometimes called the

Bamyamulenge War. Kabila arrived in Congo, recruited Congolese, and took the security forces that had fought in Angola. He and his troops then went to Kinshasa, forced President Mobutu out of power and formed a new government that lasted for about a year. In 1998, the friends of Kabila, especially the Rwandans and Ugandans, created a problem. So Kabila ran them out. That was the second war, the war of 1998.

The conflicts of Kinshasa are directly linked to Goma and other places in South Kivu. In 1998, those who left Kinshasa created a party, the Rally for Congolese Democracy (RCD), whose head is currently the vice-president of Congo. This war lasted about five years. The international community committed itself to finding a solution, resulting in the Lusaka accords and the Pretoria accords. Thanks to the international community, these accords helped Congo achieve its current unity and a certain amount of peace.

During the conflict in 1998, each of three rival factions in Congo had its own army and police force, and each tried to function as a state. Thus without officially acknowledging it, Congo was divided into three states, united only by a common national anthem. We no longer had the same currency or flag. With the peace accords, the flag, the police, the administration, and the army had to be reorganized. First, a government was formed in Kinshasa. Then the army designated new commanders and military structures in each region. The warring factions claimed various regions. South Kivu was given to the government forces, with the commander to be named by the former government. As chance would have it, the commander of the tenth military region of South Kivu was supposed to be someone from the south of Congo. But South Kivu contained a lot of Bamyamulenge soldiers who expected the regional commander to be one of them. That didn't happen because the government's appointee was to be someone who came from the Kinshasha area.

So in South Kivu we had a commander for the military region without any troops except his personal security forces, while the second in command controlled the troops. The second in command refused to submit to the commander sent by Kinshasha, and he had to return to the capital. When the government sent another commander, he and the local commander couldn't get along, so on May 16, 2004, a crisis developed between the two officers. Since it was a military crisis, bullets began to fly.

There are three phases to the crisis of military leadership in South Kivu. On May 16-18, 2004, the forces loyal to the top commander, with the help of some others, chased out most of the insurgent forces loyal to the second in command. Meanwhile the United Nations sent an observer force to position itself between the two factions and give some protection to the civilian population. Since the national commander didn't have any troops, he called on the Mai Mai to help him. These are young people who have organized themselves to defend the indigenous tribes in Congo. At first their only weapons were arrows and spears, and they believed that they could not be killed by bullets. Gradually they recovered weapons from the enemies they defeated.

The second phase of this conflict took place on May 23-28, 2004. Though the UN had created a buffer zone between the insurgents and the loyalist troops, the insurgents called on their allies in the neighboring province, North Kivu. Together these forces attacked government troops in Bukavu on May 23 and succeeded in taking over the city. The government military leaders in Kinshasa sent troops to find the defeated commander in his hiding place. The third phase of this conflict took place on May 29, when the government forces regained control over Bukavu, with the help of the troops sent from Kinshasha.

I want us to take special note of the second phase of the conflict, when for about six days the insurgents occupied the town and there was looting, raping, and killing.

During this time the insurgents went from house to house looking for American dollars and for cell phones. If you didn't have as much as ten dollars on you, you were tortured or killed. I should point out that Congo is different from perhaps all other African countries in that American currency is widely used, because our national currency has not been able to maintain much value. During the looting, the insurgents in Bukavu burned the large Kadutu market, considered the economic heart of South Kivu. After the looting, anything that remained of value was taken or was burned by the onlookers, including the food warehouses.

During the rebel occupation there was also much raping. The insurgents raped married women in the presence of their husbands and children and young women in the presence of their parents and brothers. According to reports we received via the Catholic radio station Maria, even girls younger than ten years old were raped. The rebels even required one father to rape his daughter under threat of death.

There was also much killing during this time in Bakuvu. To date we have no official death count, because many of the dead were thrown into septic tanks, local ravines, or into Lake Kivu, reminding us of the tactics in Rwanda in 1994. We will probably not know how many died until each family has come forth to identify their missing. While the insurgents were primarily responsible for the killings, even the loyalist forces committed atrocities during this time.

You can see that such events touched the entire population of South Kivu, including the Evangelical Friends Church. We are still trying to assess the damage, but our initial impression is that our people were spared from the worst of the violence. For the general population, I must say that from the moment Mobutu started to rule in 1965, his rule was characterized by very poor management and governance of the country, which really impoverished the Congolese population. Some people even say that Congo can be compared to an odd sort of heaven. While the abundance of gold, diamonds, and other natural resources might be like the beauties we can expect in heaven, if South Kivu is like heaven, the angels are poor and in fear for their very lives.

13

CRISIS IN KADUNA

Bitrus V. Z. Debki (Nigeria)

I WANT TO TELL THE STORY OF THE KADUNA CRISIS of 2000, which was a conflict about the establishment of Muslim law known as Sharia. But before telling that story, I want to give a general account of the situation before the crisis.

Between the years of 1980 and 2000, there were nineteen different crises in northern Nigeria caused by Muslims. Then after the American invasion of Afghanistan, Muslims attacked Christians in Kaduna and Kano, fighting in sympathy with their Muslim brothers in Afghanistan. When there was a problem in Iraq, they reacted in Kano. Anytime there was a problem in the southern part of Nigeria, they would take revenge on the northern Christians.

A crisis in Numan was caused by people selling water. Apparently one such person and a woman with whom he was bargaining could not agree on the price, so he beheaded the woman. In Jos, Plateau State, there was a committee called the Poverty Alleviation Committee. The governor appointed a Hausa Muslim to be the chairman. The local residents of Jos, many of whom were not Muslim, called the governor and asked him to give them a representative on the committee. Very quickly the Muslims were so belligerent that it resulted in a war. Many Christians have regarded Osama Bin Laden to be a devil, but in Nigeria you find Bin Laden t-shirts and stickers all over the Muslim region. All I'm trying to say is that Nigerian Muslims seem to be particularly aggressive. They want to fight for other Muslims and for God.

That brings us to our topic for this discussion, the Kaduna crisis. After the implementation of Sharia in Zamfara State, Muslims in the Kaduna State forwarded their own demand for Sharia to the State House of Assembly in a letter on Tuesday, December 14, 1999. The State House of Assembly appointed a committee of eleven to consider the request: five Christians, five Muslims, and the chairman, who was a Muslim. The chairman of the committee asked the Muslims to write the reasons they wanted Sharia and asked the Christians to write the reasons they didn't like Sharia. So while the committee was making an effort to collect data from people, the State House of Assembly made a move to impose Sharia on the state unconstitutionally.

The chairman of the committee, a Muslim as noted above, mobilized Muslims to march to the State House of Assembly, local government by local government. They did this for two weeks. The local government officials came one by one, and it was announced in the media that such and such local government had signed for Sharia. While this was taking place, no attention was given to members of the committee again. A plan to force Sharia to be adopted was in the pipeline. So on February 21, 2000, the Christian Association of Nigeria (CAN) organized a peaceful procession to the State House of Assembly and to the governor's house to present a letter saying we were not in support of Sharia law in Kaduna state.

For Nigerian Muslims the Sharia fight was a Jihad, a holy war, a war for God—a mandate for every Muslim to fight. It is said that anybody dying in the cause of a Jihad will immediately see God. As Christians returned from their procession to the State House of Assembly and the governor's house, the Muslims attacked them. Hundreds were killed, especially those going to the northern part of the city. The clash lasted for three days.

During this crisis there was no military intervention and no police response. The state governor knew of the plot and flew away. The deputy governor could only go up in an airplane to look at people's houses in flames. For these three days nothing was done other than killing and burning. I saw it myself. People would set the persons on fire and burn them to ashes. In the southern part of the city, Muslims were running to hide for their lives. The same was true for Christians in the northern part of the city. According to the report of Kaduna State Ministry of Works and Housing, during the February 2000 crisis, 206 churches, 105 mosques, and 8,974 houses were burned.

There was another crisis in May that year. After the February crisis, every Sunday Muslims would go to the bush as if they were going hunting. Muslim trainers would go to teach them how to shoot guns. In some places Christians did this as well. So the young people were eager to practice what they were told to learn.

Between February 23 after the first crisis and May 22, the Muslims destroyed the musical instruments of the Zion Gospel Church, but Christians did not seek revenge. On Friday, May 12, 2000, the state police commissioner had his driver take him to a mosque for prayer. He is a Muslim and his driver was a Christian. The Muslims killed the driver. Again the Christians did not seek revenge. On May 22 the Muslims killed a twenty-year-old young man named Likita Yakubu and hid the corpse inside a school building. This raised the tension level and resulted in the second crisis.

It was not easy for the Christians. At an Evangelical Church of West Africa (ECWA) congregation one Sunday morning, the youth went to the pastor and said, "Pastor, today's offering will be used to buy us guns or we leave the church. We cannot watch Muslims wipe away all Christians in Kaduna state." This led to open conflict.

After each of the crises there was a general period of regret by both Muslims and Christians. One looked around; his wife was killed. One looked around; the husband was no more. One looked around; a friend was no more. You looked around; your pastor was killed. People began to feel how terrible the situation was. The Christians under the umbrella of the Christian Association of Nigeria (CAN) were willing to enter dialogue with the Muslims. Some of the Muslims were willing to come into the dialogue, but others did not consider religion a matter for dialogue: take it or leave it.

At Jos Road, it was written on a wall, "Agree or not, Sharia must be established." At At Lagos Street by Kontagora Road, it was written on the wall, "Who owns the north?" At Zakari Road, "Sharia or war." At Abeokuta Road, "Islamic Sharia Zone—Keep off." At Shagari Road, "Sharia or Death." So dialogue became much more difficult in the city of Kaduna. However, there are some areas where Christians and Muslims did enter into dialogue, but always in fear.

After the crisis, all of the Muslims from Kaduna South were carrying their luggage and running to Kaduna North. All of the Christians in Kaduna North were running to Kaduna South. If you come to Kaduna today, Muslims are living in one place and Christians are living in another place. They do not come together again as before, except at government-reserved areas. There is a place in Kaduna where not a single Christian lives any longer. Of all churches, only one church is still standing today. In Marayi only one mosque is standing.

You can see how bad the situation between Christians and Muslims in Kaduna state has become.

As part of the reconciliation process, denominations came together for a more collective responsibility. In Nigeria we have new churches starting almost every day, and the conflict between the new churches and the existing ones is enough conflict to resolve. Some of the churches don't even attend when CAN calls for a meeting. They assume other denominations don't know that they exist. But other churches are able to come together and move as a group.

We definitely saw the love of God in those crises. Muslims used guns, even machine guns in one of the crises. In Nigeria you can buy a package of bottled beverage, drink the beverage, and throw the liter bottles anywhere you want. Some Muslims poured gasoline into a liter bottle as though it were a beverage and used it for a weapon. They set it on fire, threw the liter bottle, and once it burst, the people caught fire. Christians used sticks and stones. At the end, there was no victor, no winner. Everybody suffered.

The Church of the Brethren (EYN) in Kaduna is known as a peacemaking church, but it is in the minority there. EYN has perhaps 2,000 members within the metropolis, but there are other churches with over 300,000 members within the city. So even within the church there is some marginalization. It was difficult for us to be heard in a meeting of CAN. We could only make peace where we were active.

After the crises, the EYN church organized an offering from all the congregations as a relief fund. The Church of the Brethren in America sent relief assistance. Mission 21, based in Switzerland, also sent help. These relief materials reached all affected EYN members. We were able to help some other denominations that were helpless. So we thank God for the assistance from the COB and Mission 21 during the Kaduna crisis.

Finally, I want to stress that a common person has no security in Nigeria. Even when military men were released to go and intervene, they could not remain neutral. Muslims were killing Christian civilians for nothing, and Christians were killing Muslim civilians for nothing. They were taking revenge for their religion. Also our media are biased. If a Muslim reports the news, the impression he gives is of favoring his religion. The BBC Hausa section and the Voice of America Hausa section enlighten their listeners about how to correct problems in Nigeria. Concerning one religious problem in Gombe state, a BBC Hausa commentator said, "Muslims outnumber Christians in Gombe. Why did you allow them to cheat you? Don't agree."

If some Muslims are powerless to react, then the Muslims in Kano or Kaduna will react for them. In the Plateau State there is only one local government dominated by Muslims. The Muslims wiped out Christians from that local government. Those that survived the ugly situation ran for safety. The neighboring Christians said they would take revenge for the suffering of their Christian brethren. But a pastor stood and said, "Our faith is not like that of the Muslims. Our religion is different from theirs. Make peace. Don't fight."

This pastor then organized a dialogue between Muslims and Christians and they did achieve peace. Before anyone knew what was happening, one Sunday morning the Muslims came and surrounded the church of that very pastor while the service was being held. They poured gasoline everywhere and set the church on fire. Those who tried to escape through the windows were shot to death. Everyone in the church was killed, including the pastor. That is an example of the terrible situation between Christians and Muslims in northern Nigeria.

So I want to suggest to the Hausa sections of BBC and Voice of America that we have Christians who speak Hausa. The staff should be balanced so that each group can check the news before it is broadcast. I also want to observe that some major Christian organizations use their influence for commercial purposes and are not doing what they are supposed to do for the unity of the churches.

After the crisis in Kaduna, a panel was formed by the city government to investigate. They held two or three hearings. I was there for one of them. The Muslims controlled the panel, and as of this writing it has made no report. So in the case of Nigeria, the common person has nowhere to go to voice feelings. You can spend much time crying outside the corridors of power. No one listens to you. So people think the best way to express their feelings is to react. That's the situation in Nigeria.

14

DESTRUCTION IN KANO

Matthew Abdullahi Gali (Nigeria)

TO DENY THAT RELIGIOUS TENSION HAS EXISTED in the past as it exists in Nigeria today will serve no purpose. However, observations of religious groups among both Christians and Muslims over the last few years show that each group feels it is the one being marginalized, denied its rights, looked on with suspicion by the authorities and others. Each group has somehow developed a fortress mentality, feeling itself surrounded by enemies. Therefore, each group in turn feels that it is reasonable in its beliefs, that it is not prone to violence, that it accepts everyone on both sides.

I hope each person who sees these words will understand what I've just said. If Christians have felt discriminated against, so have Muslims. If Christians have felt that they have been unjustly treated because of their religion, so have Muslims. If Christians are feeling that they are being victimized on religious grounds, so have Muslims. I know that if you are a Christian, your first reaction may be to ask, How can Muslims feel they are being discriminated against in northern parts of Nigeria? Or if you are a Muslim, you may wonder how Christians feel their rights have been denied. Yet it is true. It is real. And it does happen.

I ask why there are divisions among Nigerians. Perhaps I may postulate a few reasons. It is said that power is a jealous mistress; that appears to be true. There are certain people who want the confusion to continue because they maintain power over people through inflaming emotions. As mentioned earlier, religion touches the core of people, so one who has religious power has great sway over others. If people begin to see one another as brothers and sisters sharing a common interest, the power base of these manipulative people will erode. Therefore, it is in their interest to keep such conflicts alive.

Certain people are maintained financially by their followers or by the exploitation of a situation in which their competitors are eliminated. If people are working together, and if healthy competitive trade builds up, certain people will lose their financial power. It benefits them to fan the fires of discord.

Another reason for keeping people apart is evident in Nigeria today, namely political power. By dividing people into different groups, either on a religious basis or a tribal basis, and encouraging them to see one another as enemies, certain elite or educated people retain their political power. People act on the words of these spokespersons rather than thinking for themselves. If people do not discuss with one another, if they do not search with others for the truth, if they do not analyze the reasons for such fears and divisions, they can easily be influenced by others who claim to be speaking for them, but who in reality are only speaking for themselves.

Churches in Kano, the EYN in particular, have endured a series of attacks from 1990 up to May 2004, when many church members were killed, maimed, and subjected to all sorts of barbaric acts at the hands of Muslim fundamentalists. However, the EYN church members were guided by Romans 12:17-21: "Do not repay anyone evil for evil, but take thought for what is noble in the sight of all." We were not shaken despite the fact that in 1991 our church was burned to ashes. In 1992 the church was burned again and bulldozed by the Kano state government through its agent called Kasseppa. In 1995 the church was burned once more by Muslim fanatics. In 2001, during the American invasion of Afghanistan in search of Osama Bin Laden, our church yet again burned down. Six people were killed on the church premises and thirty-one members lost their properties. We thank God that our overseas brothers in the Church of the Brethren, Mission 21, sent in their representative to see and hear what had transpired. They reported this information and favorable responses were received.

The EYN church and other denominations found themselves in a difficult position. It is an impossible task in this era to get land from the Kano state government for building churches. Hence Christians had to buy land from people and convert it to serve their wanted purposes. This harsh stand of the government rendered the churches vulnerable to attack by Muslim fanatics and other hooligans. May 11-13 an orgy of violence broke out in Kano in which more than 3,000 Christians and others were killed, while properties worth billions of naira were looted, destroyed, and burned. But we Christians anticipated something like this would happen, as is clearly stated in John 16:1-3: "Indeed, an hour is coming when those who kill you will think that by doing so they are offering worship to God."

Now when this violence happened, officials in Kano ordered that neither the military nor the police take action. The destruction went on for five hours. Then after many people had been killed or injured and their properties looted, a directive finally came from Abuja, from the federal government, directing the authorities to take appropriate actions. That is when the military came in and started shooting people at random.

With this situation in our minds, we went to the Kano state governor under the auspices of the Christian Association of Nigeria (CAN), of which I happened to be the first chairman from the northern states. We told the governor we were holding him responsible for the massacre of these people, and that their blood would on him. The governor insinuated that some of the CAN officials were from eastern and southern parts of Nigeria. What the Kano state governor was saying was that these CAN officials had been directed by their people in the east and the south to act on their behalf. He claimed that as far as Kano State was concerned, there were no Christians residents. Then I said, "Governor, I really am very sorry that a person in your position can deny that there are residents in Kano who are Christian. You are far from the truth." That is why we went out to inform the whole world what happened in Kano.

A reporter came from South Africa to Nigeria, and in an interview we told him what happened. There was also a French reporter who came all the way from France, and I granted him an interview as well. After four or five days I was invited by the Kano state government to defend what I had said. I repeated what I had said earlier. In fact, I even went farther because they had loaded five dump trucks with corpses and I recorded a mass burial. I told them that they had loaded those five dump trucks with corpses and buried them along Golga Road. Nobody could deny it. "You burned down people's properties," I said. "You parked the wreckage along Maidugari Road. Who authorized that? Can you deny that fact?" They could not deny it.

In conclusion I call on each and every one to pray fervently for your sisters and brothers in Nigeria, because what continues to go on is more than what has already happened. Muslims are still planning to attack Christians, not only in Kano but also in some other parts of the northern states. In the past they have held a series of night meetings every now and then, dressed in the religious garb of Nigeria. So it was possible for Christians to wear these garments and sit together with them as they discussed the whole plan in ones' presence. That is how we were alerted to what they planned. That is how we normally counteract what they plan with the authorities.

15

ETHNIC CONFLICT IN BURUNDI

David Niyonzima (Burundi)

BURUNDI HAS EXPERIENCED MULTIPLE BLOODY social political crises since it gained its independence in 1961. The dark history of our country since independence is told through the low points of killings and massacres in 1965, 1969, 1972, and 1988. While there has been substantial progress toward peace in recent years, the period from 1993 until today has been one of serious violence. All of these sad events have had an ethnic dimension, mirroring what has happened in Rwanda since its independence was granted in 1962. All the three ethnic groups in Burundi—the Hutu, Tutsi, and Twa—have been in one way or another the victims, perpetrators, and helpless spectators.

Everyone in Burundi has been impacted by and has witnessed the eruption of violence and war; sometimes lasting only a few hours, sometimes for months and years. Accompanying this violence has been great fear and sleepless nights. Because of the crisis that started in 1993, about 300,000 people have died; and 182 sites have been established for the 281,000 internally displaced people, 5.7 percent of the whole population, according to an April 2004 UNICEF report. There are 354,000 refugees from Burundi who live in Tanzania. So widespread has the recent violence and displacement been that the life expectancy has fallen from 53 to 39. The human development index of the United Nations Development Program (UNDP) positions Burundi at 171 out of 174 countries, making it the third poorest country in the world.

With this overview of the recent history of Burundi you can imagine how strongly people need peacebuilding, healing, forgiveness, and renewal. And considering the many similarities with the situation in Rwanda and the many ways in which the two cultures and political systems interact with each other, there is much to be discouraged about in the beautiful Great Lakes region of central Africa.

THE AFRICAN CHURCHES' GIFT TO THE WORLD
ANN RIGGS (USA)

One of the most important insights from this volume is an awareness of how much the churches in Africa have to offer other churches around the world struggling with these issues in their settings. African Christians have found hope that they can pass along to churches in South America, where I know they need hope, and churches in Asia, where they also need hope. This is a gift the Africans can give to other churches who may feel alone and who think no other church has ever faced the kinds of struggles that they are facing. Of course, situations are all different, but the gift of hope is one that can be sent from Africa to Christians around the world.

16

ASSASSINATION IN BURUNDI

Philippe Nakuwundi (Burundi)

BURUNDI IS BORDERED BY RWANDA TO THE NORTH, the Democratic Republic of the Congo to the west, and Tanzania to the east and south. Its population is currently about 7,000,000. Ninety percent of the population is agrarian, and the same number consider themselves Christian in some sense. In addition to Kirundi, the national language, we use French as our educational and administrative language, one of the remnants of Belgian rule. Swahili is widely used as a trade language, since it is used in so much of East and Central Africa.

Burundi has been deeply troubled since its independence. Recurring ethnic conflicts have repeatedly plunged our country into mourning, both for the casualties and the separation of families as people have fled into exile. Among the most alarming of these conflicts have been those of 1965, 1968, 1972, 1987, and 1991. Unfortunately the most dramatic of the conflicts has been the one that began in 1993 and has lasted well into the twenty-first century. This most recent round of violence began with the assassination of President Melchior Ndadaye, the first democratically elected president and a Hutu, who had only been in office for three months.

President Melchior's assassination had serious consequences on a variety of levels, including the proliferation of armed groups and the continuation of government instability. On the social level, the

99

general insecurity throughout the country has provoked population displacement externally and internally. The hope for cooperation between the ethnic groups was poisoned by divisive ideologies on both sides, and matters in this regard remain very, very difficult. On the economic level, the civil war has caused major disruption in schools, hospitals, and businesses. On the psychological level, the horror of this war has so traumatized many Burundians that they are skeptical about political initiatives and pessimistic about the future in general.

Despite all of this, there is a glimmer of hope on the horizon. Today hostilities have ceased in 95 percent of the republic as a result of the signing of the Pretoria peace accords between the main armed movements and the government. With this agreement, Burundi is beginning to look at issues such as the demobilization of ex-combatants, the return or repatriation of more than 500,000 external refugees, the reintegration of more than 500,000 internally displaced persons, the democratization of institutions, and the general reconstruction of the country. We have a big challenge ahead of us. We in Burundi have managed to hold things together for four decades, so there is considerable optimism about the future.

17

GENOCIDE IN RWANDA

Cecile Nyiramana (Rwanda)

RWANDA, MY COUNTRY, IS SMALL AND AMONG the poorest countries of the world. Unfortunately, we are in competition with our neighbor to the south, Burundi, for that distinction. And like Burundi, our country has experienced many ethnic struggles. For example, just before independence an outbreak of violence caused much death and many exiles. In 1973 another period of ethnic strife led to a substantial number of deaths and exiles. The groups of refugees from violence in 1959 and 1973 began to organize themselves to oppose the forces in Rwanda and to prepare for war. In 1990 war began, lasting until 1994. That is the period I will focus on.

Many already know about the events of 1994, for the genocide has become the one thing most people of the world know about our tiny country. The violence began in April and lasted until July, about 100 days. There was enormous loss of lives for such a short time, about one million, a substantial percentage of our population. Among those who escaped death were many who were wounded and many others who were traumatized and lost hope for a more peaceful future. Those who managed to escape the country did not escape the trauma and despair, for we know how important to Africans is their place of birth and being with loved ones. It is no exaggeration to say that all Rwandans were traumatized in some way by the genocide.

The identification of the events of 1994 as genocide involves more than just the huge number of deaths and the universal trauma. The violence was not political or geographic, it was ethnic. The world community has come to recognize the ways in which Rwandan genocide is similar to horrible genocides at other places in the past. It has taken ten years for some to understand this, but it seems to be well recognized now, and that itself gives us Rwandans some hope.

As I have said, the effects of the genocide went far beyond the killings. There were a number of women raped, many houses destroyed, and property looted. This left us with a large number of orphans, widows, and people who were arbitrarily imprisoned, charged with being involved in the genocide. We have about 120,000-130,000 people still in prison, and despite efforts to use traditional justice practices to hear their cases, the number has not been reduced very much. Many of those who were severely traumatized continue to experience psychological, social, and economic problems. Relationships between neighbors were destroyed, so we have had to reconstruct these relationships, especially between those who survived the genocide and those presumed guilty of violence.

18

FEAR AND MARGINALIZATION IN ETHIOPIA

Million Belete (Ethiopia)

ETHIOPIA IS MENTIONED IN THE BIBLE MANY TIMES. In some places it is referred to as Cush. Some people say that the eunuch mentioned in Acts 8:26-39 was from Nubia in the Sudan, and not from Ethiopia. I would only point out that Ethiopia has been fragmenting for many years, so both Cush and Nubia were probably in the same general area. Ten years ago, when my wife was asked, "In which country were you born?" she would say, "I was born in Ethiopia." If you ask her today, she would say "I was born in Eritrea." So the story goes. Our country has not been colonized as such, so I can't say we became independent from other nations. There were attempts to colonize us, but we stopped them. Black power defeated white power, and they went away.

Today there is an aspect of our story that we are both proud and ashamed of. We are proud that Christianity came to Ethiopia before it went to Europe and America. But we are ashamed that Ethiopia did not send missionaries to the rest of Africa to proclaim the gospel of Christ. In 1960 Billy Graham came to Ethiopia and said, "You should have been the ones to send missionaries all over Africa, but you didn't." He was right. Our country is referred to as an "island of

Christianity," that is, a Christian nation surrounded by Muslim countries. In a religious sense we are predominantly two groups: Christians and Muslims.

Mennonites came to Ethiopia at the end of the World War II for humanitarian purposes, then they continued as missionaries. They came to teach us, to teach us our own book. You know that in the book of Acts the eunuch was reading a book—but where did he get that book? It was his book. The same is true in my own life, because the Mennonites came to teach me my own book. I came to know the Lord Jesus Christ through the teaching of a missionary. He used to stand in front of us and teach. He would put a question on the blackboard and say, "Go to the Bible and find the answer for this." Many of the questions he asked were my own questions, and I would say, "I don't want the answers from this white man. I want the answers from my book." So I would go and study from my book.

The dark period in our church's history was 1974-1991, when there was a Marxist government in our country. Our church was closed and we went underground. When we went underground, our church consisted of twelve congregations and maybe 5,000 members. When the Marxist government was overthrown, we came out from underground and discovered that the membership had grown to 50,000. The number of congregations had multiplied many times. In Addis Ababa alone, when we went underground, there was only one congregation. When we came out, they had organized themselves into six congregations. Today in Addis Ababa alone there are nineteen congregations. We thank God for the growth. Much has happened.

These dark periods were of course times when Christians in Ethiopia, especially the evangelical churches, came closer together. Our current problem and our primary prayer concern is the Eritrean war. It has affected all of us, including my family. My wife was born in Eritrea, so the problem is very near to us. It has very much affected our whole land. We are afraid of what will happen. We have learned a lot from the other peace churches. The prayer concern I present is the fact that in our country today, the political system is promoting politics along ethnic lines. Our government has told us to organize ourselves according to our ethnic identity. On my identification card, my ethnicity is plainly written. This is not good; it could become a very serious problem.

We have seen what has happened to other countries organized along ethnic lines. We have seen what happened in Zimbabwe, and we know what happened there could happen in Ethiopia. We all know what happened in Rwanda, and we hope and pray that what happened there will not happen in Ethiopia. We know that what happened in Rwanda was due to its being organized along tribal lines. Recently when I was in Rwanda, I heard that in Rwanda no one may speak of tribal identities. The two words *Tutsi* and *Hutu* are taboo. They told me, "We don't speak in that way to anyone; we are all Rwandans." That's what we want to happen in our country in the future.

I also want to say that the evangelical churches in Ethiopia are speaking to the issues of peace and justice. We in Ethiopia enjoy the freedom to preach as we wish, yet we are still marginalized. Since our population is 15-20 percent evangelical Christians, we are considered a minority, and consequently injustice is done to us. Most of our congregations in Ethiopia do not have a church building.

As I mentioned, there are nineteen congregations in Addis Ababa, but only one worships in a building. The rest worship in sheds. The Muslims, the Ethiopian Orthodox Christians, and the Roman Catholics are fully recognized by the government. Evangelical Christians must have government permission to exist. Until last year, this permission had to be renewed every year. The period for which we may register has now been increased to three years. We are also praying that this will be granted to us.

19

THE SITUATION IN SUDAN

Harold Miller (USA)

This material first appeared in the Mennonite Central Committee Peace Office Newsletter as *"Peace and Pain in Sudan," vol 35, no. 2 (April-June, 2005), pp. 1-5. Used here by permission of the MCC Peace Office.*

SUDAN, AFRICA'S LARGEST COUNTRY BY AREA, is host to the world's largest humanitarian crisis, so declared (before the December 2004 Asian tsunami) by the United Nations. This crisis is focused in Darfur, a region in Western Sudan the size of Kenya where an estimated 1.6 million of its citizens are designated as internally displaced people (IDPs).

But the Darfur region is only the most recent flash point attracting international attention to this vast country. South Sudan, demarcated by a 1956 colonial "boundary," is just emerging from decades of civil war that resulted in the deaths of an estimated 2.5 million people and in the displacement or exile of millions more.

Today Sudan is attempting, at once, to contain a burgeoning conflict in Darfur and to manage an impending peace for south Sudan. Together, these disparate dynamics provide entry points for a consideration of the country's torturous political, religious, and economic circumstances.

BACKGROUND

Sudan is situated in north/central Africa, with a coast on the Red Sea. It bridges desert and tropical forests, Africa and the Middle East, Arabs and Africans, Muslims and Christians, subsistence livelihoods and modern oil production. How can Sudan's diversities be integrated into a cohesive modern state? Are its integration issues to be addressed by African statecraft; by Islamic, Middle Eastern, or Arab polity; or by a combination of these?

Without recourse to the annals of history, current events in Sudan remain opaque and inaccessible. Constant to the story of Sudan is the theme of violence and conflict, instigated and sustained by the quest for human chattel from southern Sudan for markets in the Middle East, by the tension between imposed foreign/in-country governance systems, on the one hand and modern notions of self-determination, on the other.

One of the reference points in Sudan's modern history is the year 1821, when the Turko-Egyptian (Ottoman) administration claimed much of today's Sudan. In so doing, the Ottomans brought some semblance of perverse "order" to a thriving slave trade, which had until then functioned in a geographic and economic free-for-all.

By 1881 nationalist sentiments flared into an armed revolt against the Ottoman administration, instigated by a "Mahdi" (Muhammed Ahmed el Mahdi, "the sent one") a revivalist Sudanese Muslim patriot who achieved Sudan's first short-lived sovereignty. In 1898, the Mahdi's successor was overthrown by the British Lord Kitchener and replaced by the Anglo-Egyptian Condominium government, which ruled until Sudan's independence in 1956.

In 1955 southern soldiers of the Sudanese army staged a mutiny that led to a civil war between the government of Sudan (GoS) and the Anya Nya, a rebel movement led by General Joseph Lagu. Together with other rebel southern Sudanese, he objected to the lesser status accorded to south Sudan and to the prospect that this would continue after independence.

In the wake of the rebellion, a seventeen-year civil war persisted until 1972, when Canon Burgess Carr of Liberia, then General Secretary of the All Africa Conference of Churches (AACC), with Emperor Haile Selassie of Ethiopia as witness, brokered the Addis Ababa Peace Agreement. Relative peace prevailed in Sudan for nearly a decade, only to be disrupted when Sudan's President Numeri abrogated the agreement, igniting the second phase of the civil war. Colonel John Garang, a Sudanese Army defector, led the southern rebel forces known as the Sudan People's Liberation Movement/Army (SPLM/A), during the second phase.

By the early 1990s the SPLM/A had achieved a military stalemate with the GoS's armed forces and felt pressure from various quarters, including Sudanese churches, to negotiate a settlement from this position of strength. But just as such negotiations were about to commence, the SPLM/A was convulsed by an internal leadership wrangle, thus forfeiting most of its military gains. The rebel war was renewed but rendered vastly more complex as the leadership struggle persisted.

By 1993, the civil war in south Sudan was affecting cities in northern Sudan, Sudan's neighbors, and the larger world. Refugees from south Sudan were exiting across the borders while mass displacement was taking place within the country. Nearly half the population of the capital, Khartoum, eventually consisted of displaced southerners, many of them Christians. For both northern and southern Sudanese, it was an unprecedented and uncomfortable situation.

THE PEACE PROCESS

In response to this conflagration, the governments of Kenya, Uganda, Ethiopia, Djibouti, Eritrea, Sudan, and Somalia established a special secretariat in the early 1990s within the existing Inter-Governmental Authority for Development (IGAD) to negotiate peace between the GoS and the SPLM/A.

During the following decade, the peace process sauntered along, with the protagonists abusing it to their respective propagandist advantage. But with the shock of September 11, the related U.S. focus on Sudan as a terrorist haven, and the prospect of oil exports from south Sudan, there was growing pressure to move the peace process forward. By late 2003 the vice president of Sudan and the SPLA/M leader—both deemed intractable hardliners—became the primary negotiators within the framework. Following this dramatic shift in the profile of the negotiators, the peace process quickly accelerated.

By May 2004, the GoS and the SPLM/A had signed six protocols as precursors to a comprehensive peace agreement. The reelection in November 2004 of George W. Bush and the extraordinary meeting in the same month of the United Nations Security Council (UNSC) in Nairobi, Kenya, together sustained pressure on the negotiations. The protagonists agreed during the UNSC meeting that the GoS and the

SPLA/M would sign a peace accord by the end of 2004. In the event, an accord was signed on January 9, 2005, in Nairobi, Kenya.

This peace agreement provides for a popular referendum to be called within six years of its signing to review the progress made toward implementation of the peace. It also provides south Sudan with an option to secede from the country.

THE DARFUR CRISIS

Meanwhile, the Darfur region, in the west of the country, was experiencing a growing military confrontation between the GoS and three Darfurian rebel groups: the Sudan Liberation Movement (SLM), the Joint Equity Movement (JEM), and the splinter Reform and Development Movement (RDM). The conflict so far has claimed an estimated 70,000 lives and caused internal displacement of 1.6 million people as well as the departure of several hundred thousand refugees to Chad.

Basic to the tension in Darfur is competition between farmers of African origin in the south and pastoralists of Afro-Arab origin migrating seasonally from northern Darfur. While the northern desert is expanding, both population groups are also expanding and requiring more land. Although both Arab and African communities of Darfur are Muslim, the African farmer communities claim that the GoS is promoting a policy of cultural Arabization, thus favoring the pastoralists.

In 2003, the grievances of the African community in Darfur escalated and took the form of two and then three armed rebel groups. The predictable response of the GoS was to provide arms and logistical support for the Arab pastoralists, widely referred to as the Janjaweed, or armed horsemen.

Negotiations regarding a possible cease-fire between the rebels and the GoS are ongoing in Abuja, Nigeria, under the auspices of the African Union, Africa's political continental umbrella. The parties have agreed to the distribution of humanitarian assistance to displaced people within Darfur and to a provisional ceasefire. Meanwhile the UN's special representative to Sudan, Jan Pronk, claims western Darfur no longer responds to the authority of the GoS or its surrogates, the Janjaweed.

In response to strong international pressure, the GoS has permitted humanitarian agencies to deliver relief aid even as Sudan's President Beshir accuses faith-based agencies of exploiting the plight of

Darfurians for proselytizing purposes. The negotiations in Nigeria have been recessed until early 2005, while armed conflict continues and aid workers are being killed. As of this writing, the United Nations Security Council is considering the imposition of sanctions against the GoS for its role in the Darfur debacle.

DARFUR IN HISTORY

In the 1600s, Darfur was an independent sultanate. The sultanate survived until the 1890s, when the Condominium government integrated it into the larger Sudan. With independence in 1956, the GoS insisted that Darfur continue as part of Sudan, much to the resentment of Darfurians. Afro-Arab Darfurians to this day sustain the memory of the famous Darfurian, Muhammed Ahmed al Mahdi, who in 1881 established Sudan as a politically independent Islamic entity. At the, time, the Mahdi had advised his followers that Africans with their land, wives, and livestock were "there for the taking" in fulfilment of his mission of the "sent one."

As a religiously motivated patriot, the Mahdi was greatly exercised by the compromised nature of the Ottoman administration of the Sudan, at the head of which was General Charles Gordon, the Christian British military general. According to popular legend, Gordon was speared to death on the steps of Khartoum's state house by the Mahdi's followers in what was considered a miraculous victory over Ottoman rule.

As a Muslim revivalist, the Mahdi (and his successor, the Khalifa) was committed to the propagation of orthodox Sunni Islam in Sudan. In pursuit of this goal, the Mahdiyya state administered Sharia rule, with the most dire economic and social consequences. In 1898 the British replaced the Mahdiyya with the Anglo-Egyptian Condominium government, leading to a reassertion and expansion of Sufi Islam. These respective poles are represented in Sudanese politics today by the Umma Party, led by a direct descendant of the Mahdi, and the Democratic Unionist Party (DUP), with its Egyptian connections.

After the upheavals of the late 1880s, Sudan settled for the praxis of a moderate Sufi Islam which was assaulted in 1989 when the current government came to power, after a long gestation period nurtured and guided by Dr. Hassan el Turabi, a Sudanese political ideologue (of Nigerian ancestry) with longstanding relationships with the Egyptian Muslim Brotherhood, advocates for a strong Islamic manifesto. Under his tutelage, Sudan was declared a Muslim state and promoted itself as a beachhead for spreading Islamic faith throughout Africa.

Turabi's political agenda and that of his ruling colleagues eventually diverged, with Turabi being ousted from the government, imprisoned, and publicly tried for challenging Sudan's ruling clique—which since 1956 has been drawn almost exclusively from Dongola, northern Sudan. In his ascent to power, Turabi had made opportunist cause with politically marginal groups such as the African farmers in Darfur and the SPLM/A. He has been sidelined, but the effects of his political muscle have not been fully quelled.

SPLM/A head, John Garang (now deceased), spoke much of including all of the country's marginalized peoples in a unified Sudan and suggested repeatedly that the recently signed peace accord (Jan. 2005) could serve as a blueprint toward resolution of the problems in Darfur. Interestingly, this possibility was reported as a "sticking issue" in the final negotiations.

In the final analysis, the upheavals in Sudan have been about who benefits from and who controls the country's considerable resources, including oil. As master strategist in a complex political contest, Turabi was widely perceived to have played the religion card in opportunist fashion. In fact, the most intense debates about religion in Sudan have occurred within Muslim-Muslim rather than in Muslim-Christian discussions. Religio-political dynamics in Sudan have much in common with the larger Middle East, where active civil society groups challenge the ruling elite.

PART IV

STORIES OF CHRISTIAN PEACEMAKING

Stories that emphasize what the Historic Peace Churches have done internally in response to violence

20

HEALING, FORGIVENESS, AND RECONCILIATION

David Niyonzima (Burundi)

OUR CHURCH IS SMALL, but we have sought to work at peacemaking. In 1999 several of us organized a meeting in Bujumbura dealing with conscientious objection. It brought together churches from Burundi, Rwanda, and Congo, the churches known as Historic Peace Churches. We gained from the insights of those from as far away as Colombia and Guatemala. Then there was another meeting held in Nairobi in which we attempted to set up a network of communication between the Historic Peace Churches in the African Great Lakes region.

Unfortunately we weren't able to continue with this initiative until 2004, when David Bucura, a Friends leader from Rwanda, organized another meeting similar to the one we had previously. Held in Kigali in April, it was very productive. We decided to set up an ongoing forum for the Historic Peace Churches of Africa and established three main objectives. The first was to lobby against the proliferation of small arms. The second was to establish the culture of peace through a peace theology. The third was to advocate for human rights and peaceful resolution of conflicts.

Building peace continually involves healing, forgiveness, and renewal. These have been challenging issues for me, because I have been struggling with them in my own life. A year ago I was put in jail

115

for refusing to hand over the keys to our church's vehicles as we were amid a contentious change of leadership in the Friends Church in Burundi. I won't tell the whole story, but suffice it to say that I was deeply wounded and offended. I was harassed, abused, and tortured psychologically. As this was happening, I began to wonder if the message of peace, love, and justice my church had been advocating was a dream that would ever come true. I was released, thanks to a few close friends of mine who spoke on my behalf to the supervisor of the one who had arrested me.

When I was asked to write about this topic, I struggled, not knowing how I could present my views in a way that would really spring from my heart and express my optimism that we are advocating for a noble, achievable cause. As I sat down to write, I felt as if God was directing me to the words of Jesus when people asked him who could be saved. It was after his disciples witnessed the event of the conversation between Jesus and a rich ruler that they realized it was hard for the rich man to "sell everything" he had so that he might have treasures in heaven.

Then Jesus said, in Luke 18:27, "What is impossible with men, is possible *with God*" (NIV), and I want to underline the phrase "with God." I was energized by this Scripture and the belief that peace is possible "with God" and that we have a role to play. Our peace testimony over the years as peace churches has never changed, even though it has met many challenges. It will continue to make an impact on society regardless of the different forces attempting to shake it.

We in the peace churches believe peace begins in a relationship with Christ. I mean peace with God in heart and mind. Establishing a relationship with Christ brings peace within, because Christ brings order into an individual's life. This peace within must be interactive and interdependent. It must be both spiritual and social. It must be spiritual, as Paul says in Romans 5:1: "Therefore, since we are justified by faith, we have peace with God through our Lord Jesus Christ." It must be social also as Paul says in 1 Thessalonians 5:13: "Be at peace among yourselves." In 2 Corinthians 13:11 we read: "Aim for perfection, listen to my appeal, be of one mind, live in peace" (NIV).

Peace with the creation is the part of peace often neglected. When there was war in Burundi, displaced people took over some of the mountainous areas and lived in them. As a result, these places have been destroyed. In the forest where the rebels have stayed, animals have nearly been exterminated. Howard Zehr, director of the Conflict Transformation Program at Eastern Mennonite University, says that

"Wrongdoing violates shalom." Shalom, according to Zehr "is to live together in right relationship with our creator, each other, and with creation."

Emphasizing right relationships is already a part of our culture. In Africa we all know that people are who they are because of others. I heard a proverb among the Zulus of South Africa which says, "*Umuntu ngumuntu ngabantu,*" meaning "A person is a person through persons." A similar concept is found among the Banyamulenge of the Eastern Democratic Republic of Congo. These people, who speak Kinyarwanda because of their Rwandan origin, say, "*Umuntu umwe si ikibira,*" which means "One tree is not a forest."

Following this logic, it becomes clear that my peace depends on others being at peace. That is why I say peace should be interdependent. Countries are beginning to understand that their security does not depend on their strong internal order, defense forces, and policies. They know a war in neighboring countries will easily flow into their own territory in the form of refugees with many needs.

In Burundi, even though there have been bloody events for decades, we have the tradition of peacebuilding through the system of *Abashingantahe* or the eldership. In Rwanda they have the *Gacaca*, which is the traditional court system. We know that these systems have worked historically, but the traditional practices and values have been distorted by the prevalence of violence in our culture today.

Peace as we in the Historic Peace Churches understand it is not temporal or short-lived. It is peace that is from God, peace that comes not only when people have signed a peace accord or when the guns have stopped blasting. In Rwanda the genocide started on April 7, 1994, exactly when the airplane carrying presidents Havyarimana Juvenal and Cyprien Ntaryamira was hit by a missile. They were coming from Arusha, where a peace accord had just been signed, and ironically they were returning with good news. But their assassination became the horrible trigger for an unprecedented period of violence. The kind of peace that our churches would like to promote is the peace that lasts. It is peace based on biblical principles such as love, kindness, forgiveness, mercy, justice, tolerance, and patience.

Reflecting on the traditional system of peacemaking in Burundi, I emphasize that those who were asked to be in it were persons motivated to help those in conflict, wanting to understand why they were quarreling and fighting. I have written about this in my book, *Unlock-*

ing Horns (Barclay Press, 2001) about how these people were operating: "Thanks to their wisdom on numerous occasions they averted potential frontier wars between chiefdoms, quarrels between rival royal family members, and major disputes among families" (p. 29).

The *mushingantahe* was called on in the traditional culture because of his peace-mindedness, honesty, transparency, and concern for the welfare of the community. But today the traditional practice of peacemaking has been lost for the most part, and this is a great loss to us. Some say in Kirundi *"Ababipfa n'ababisangiye,"* which means "Those who fight are those who have things in common." They go their way, everybody has become so busy with his or her own affairs and everybody is "getting late to his or her program." They say, "My agenda did not include these issues today."

When I was a small boy, I used to hear people clearing their throats at the gate of our village compound as they greeted my father early in the morning on their way down to the valley to work in their gardens. I will never forget a man called Masunzu to whom my father had given a number of plots of land in our valley—where he planted cabbage, carrots, and tomatoes. During summer holidays I always heard him, not far from our gate, calling *"Mwake, mwake"* which means "good morning, good morning," whether there was somebody to respond or not. I heard him before I woke up and always knew that we had a good sunny, peaceful day because Masunzu had traveled six kilometers from his home to come and work in his gardens.

This is a wonderful memory of those peaceful days in Burundi. Some people, like Masunzu, would call and sometimes wait for a response to which they would always say things like, "It was so and so passing by the gate, wondering if you had woken up in peace." Such traditions must be revived and once again take root in people's relationships.

The legacy of peacemaking is not only ours to possess but also to pass on to our children. There will be a time when our children will want to know what their parents and grandparents left behind for them, such as the legacy of actions appropriate when they get into difficult situations. Since conflicts are inevitable, we must know how to resolve the differences peacefully instead of using weapons to destroy each other.

We are also to avoid the spirit of vengeance, because vengeance brings about a vicious cycle of killing that will never end. This is probably the cause of the endless war in our region. We must promote forgiveness. It was Geiko Muller Fahrenholz who said in his book *The Art of Forgiveness* that "Much more than a word or gesture, forgiveness is a genuine process of encounter of healing of releasing of new options for the future" (WCC Publications, Geneva, 1997, p. 5).

In the late 1990s two outspoken men in Burundi considered each other to be enemies, even though they had never met each other. One was a powerful politician, the other a rich business man. The politician, being a Hutu, used his political influence to organize Hutu militia to be ready to attack Tutsi militia in defense of Hutu intellectuals. The businessman funded Tutsi militia to defend against the Hutus. In other words, the two men were fighting each other indirectly. Also, each had heard about the other one as a person who could kill him at first sight, if given the opportunity. They were afraid of each other, even though they had never met.

One day the two men happened to be traveling to Nairobi at the same time. For those who have been to Burundi, you know Burundi is not blessed with numerous flight choices. In fact, there was a time when only one airline came to Burundi, and planes arrived only once a week. It so happened that the two men were seated together, and it must have been God's plan. People saw them together and were shocked, since it was common knowledge that they were enemies. But these two "enemies" had actually never met, so they didn't even notice the puzzlement of the others on the flight.

After the flight was underway, they decided to introduce themselves. You can imagine their complete shock on discovering that each was chatting with his own worst enemy. But because they felt they had no choice but to continue talking during the remainder of the flight, they began to talk about their hatred for each other.

This all may seem implausible, but it actually happened. To make a long story short, they not only talked about the issues they had with each other, but they forgave each other and walked off the plane as friends, not enemies. What a miracle! Today they are still good friends, both involved with the prayer breakfast movement that has been gathering political figures and other prominent personalities together to address the spiritual and political aspects of peace and reconciliation.

According to Gayle Leonore Macnab's notes for the 2003 Seminar on Trauma and Recovery, forgiveness

> opens the heart of the victim to communicate with God; it re-focuses the mind and the heart of the victim on the journey to healing; it softens the heart of the victim to receive God's love and

mercy and healing; it releases the need and desire for revenge; it
releases the responsibility of the victim for administering judgment; it allows for renewed hope, opens the heart to receive love,
and renews the ability to trust; it creates the ability to choose a
different response than anger, pain, fear, and revenge.

This is wonderful teaching and so important for Burundi.

There was a time during our national crisis when young people,
manipulated by extremist politicians and businessmen set about to
do what they called "The dead city operations." During these operations the youth put barricades in the streets of Bujumbura to prevent
people from going to work. They also went about killing people they
thought were of the opposite ethnic group. It was terrible, and many
people died, especially in the suburbs near the university where
youth gangs called *"Sans echeque et Sans defaite"* (without failure and
without defeat) operated.

Peggy (not her real name) is a widow living in Bujumbura, and
she gave us this testimony during one of our peace workshops. Her
son was part of these Without Defeat killings. One day she asked her
son if he knew how to distinguish a Hutu from a Tutsi physically. Her
son answered hesitantly because he was not sure how, since the
killing for the youth was more of a game than a political endeavor.

She asked her son if he knew whether he himself was a Hutu or a
Tutsi. Her son paused and asked her if he wasn't a Tutsi. When Peggy
asked him if he knew his father, her son got even more confused and
looked down. Peggy told her son that since he did not know his father, he could be a Hutu killing his own. Her son decided to ask for
forgiveness, because it dawned on him that what he was doing was
against his mother's wishes and could have been aimed at his father's
relatives.

To bring about healing, we need to promote opportunities for
people to express themselves as others listen compassionately. Active
listening heals. War has caused people to get sick, even if they do not
realize it. Those of us who have been affected by war and conflict
need healing. The healing process will take effect when people start
opening up to each other in safe environments and really listening to
each other. We have seen this and we have seen how it is possible
through the ministry of the Trauma Healing and Reconciliation Services (THARS) that I am involved with in Burundi. Active listening
sounds simple and easy, but this is one of the cures for trauma and a
key for fostering renewal. We should not minimize each other's problems and concerns.

When there is conflict we must find a way to talk about it. Politicians call it dialogue. Nelson Mandela used the process of dialogue in February 2000 at Arusha with the Burundi party leaders. It worked. There were politicians there who had not met for a long time, because some lived in Burundi and some lived outside Burundi. They listened to each other, they talked to each other, and in the evening it was amazing to see them sharing glasses of wine together. We have a saying in Kirundi, *"Ubika mu nda ugatarura ibiboze,"* which means, "If you keep something in the stomach, it will make you sick." This is a way of saying that it is very dangerous not to express what is on your mind. Over recent years our organization has been training people and facilitating active listening for hundreds of traumatized victims through our listening rooms. I believe all members of the Historic Peace Churches must be a channel of God's healing power to the wounded, oppressed, discriminated against, rejected, and abused.

Near Kibimba, a small village in Burundi, lives Rachel (not her real name). She is young and married, with two children. Rachel's husband, who is quite a bit older than her, is in prison for torturing her. He was experiencing sexual performance difficulties, blamed the problem on her, and to punish her attacked her with a machete. Rachel was nearly killed. He aimed to decapitate her, but his swing was too high. Now she has a wound from the back of her head through her right ear and on to her right cheek. She also has a wound on her right hand that nearly splits her thumb from the rest of her hand and a scar on her right shoulder that runs vertically to the middle of her back.

Rachel nearly died that day, then barely survived a long hospital stay complicated by poverty. Her husband was prosecuted, and for a long time she could not even begin to talk about what had happened to her. Someone eventually suggested that she visit the listening room that had recently opened in her community. During her first session with the listener, she could do nothing but cry. Over time, with encouragement and support, she was able to get her story out and gain release from her traumatic memories. Recently she was able to tell her story to a group of women at the healing workshop we organized. This educated the women and empowered Rachel.

In Makamba (not his real home) there is a man who was the pastor of a local church. He had some very normal conflicts with some leaders of his church. As a result of these he ended up leaving the church and starting another. His new church did well, but his former church elders decided to get rid of him. They signed a paper denouncing him to the local military as a rebel. He was arrested and tortured. His torture included being tied up and hung for an entire night. He was beaten numerous times, which knocked out his teeth and left him very bloody. His torment ended only when another church leader intervened and got him transferred to another city. There he received a trial and was acquitted of all charges.

This pastor found the listening rooms by attending a local healing seminar we sponsored. As he listened, he realized he was in great need of these services himself. He stayed afterward, spoke to the organizer, and was given an appointment. He was given much-needed medical attention and psychotherapy. In one of his psychotherapy sessions he told us his healing was enabling him to forgive those who had tortured him.

In Gitega a twenty-eight-year-old woman was raped by soldiers. She bore a child from this rape but had great difficulty adjusting to being its mother. While the child was still young, government soldiers attacked her family compound; she witnessed the execution of her parents and siblings. She was the last to be attacked and only survived because the soldier who was attacking her said, "I am tired, I have been killing people all day, I want to quit." This woman is now receiving extensive therapy at our center.

A central part of peacemaking is the implementation of restorative justice. In his book *Restorative Justice: Rebirth of an Ancient Practice* (MCC Canada, 1994, p. 7), Martin Wright says, "Evil is balanced in offering a support to the victim and inquiring from the perpetrator a conversation with the help of the community when necessary." He points out that the community must be renewed by the power of the Holy Spirit to get involved in restoring relationships.

Lasting peace is that in which the whole community is involved, a situation in which people do not accuse each other but seek to collectively find ways of restoring relationships. In healing of relationships the approach should be to encourage the community to realize the wrong has been committed against the community, not just against an individual. In Burundi, as in other African cultures, the culture is communally oriented. A crime or shameful act against one person is felt or mourned by the whole community. This is why there is a proverb in Kirundi that says *Umuryambwa aba umwe agatukisha umuryango,* meaning "A person who eats a dog turns the whole family into dog eaters." Because of this, in restoring relationships the whole village must be involved. And we who are members of Historic Peace Churches must consider ourselves as a new village.

In Rwanda, Gacaca, a pre-colonial court system, uses panels through which truth is revealed publicly in a village setting. Rwandans believe truth-telling and confession are what will heal their country. In fact the country is working at setting up as many as 90,000 Gacaca courts. The big point here is the involvement of the community and the knowledge that the task of bringing such a big number of people to trial cannot possibly be done in a Western-style court system. They realize the need for a system in which the community is deeply involved.

Building peace is possible, and we know it because what is impossible with men is possible with God. For reasons I do not fully understand, God chooses to work with human beings to achieve what looks unachievable. Also I would like to stress that I believe forgiveness is what will heal our countries. We who are members of the Historic Peace Churches must be at the forefront in this endeavor. We must live out our peace testimony practically. We know that when we are reconciled with God and with ourselves, peace will overflow to our neighbors and even to the creation. We must redouble our efforts to support the initiatives of peacebuilding, forgiveness, healing, and renewal. We must work together, all of us who believe our weapons for war should be turned into plowshares and pruning forks. We are in this together; we should support each other, uphold each other, and never give up.

21

HEALING IN BURUNDI

Philippe Nakuwundi (Burundi)

THE CONFLICTS IN BURUNDI SINCE 1965 have been difficult for the Evangelical Friends Church. In 1972, many of our people were coldly murdered, and others had to flee into exile. We lost many of our leaders that year, since the killings targeted those with education and in positions of leadership. In a later episode of violence, our leaders were once again singled out. Eight students in the pastoral school at Kwibuka were found dead on this sad, sad occasion. These were not just young people with future potential; these were experienced pastors seeking to strengthen their skills.

Because of the loss of so many leaders, and because the problems of ethnic and political conflict are so central to the gospel in Burundi, in 1999 the Friends yearly meetings in the Great Lakes area joined to together to establish the Great Lakes School of Theology. Its mission is to train leaders for the churches and to prepare people to be peacemakers in the Great Lakes region. In fact, I am a graduate of this Bible college and a beneficiary of its mission.

Besides these training efforts, other activities have developed, but often with great difficulty. Since 1972, succeeding governments have reduced the public space and the public forums for our people and our churches in Burundi. This was demonstrated most obviously by the closing of several Christian churches in 1976. This situation continued until the eve of the 1992 elections. So during this period the Friends Church in Burundi, like many other churches, was reduced to near-silence on the conflict issues' absence from the debate on peace-making.

The events of 1993 unleashed another blow to the people's hope to live in a peaceful democracy. Despite such discouragement, the Friends Church began to play a more active role in restoring peace and calming the people.

Take, for example, one of our larger churches in Kibimba: Before 1993, there had been a large compound there, housing the church headquarters, our hospital, the missionary station, and the secondary and primary schools. Kibimba was systematically destroyed in the violence of 1993. The surrounding areas experienced much loss of life, beginning with the death of about seventy students burned alive at a gas station. The chaos continued until the center of town was transformed into a refuge camp. From then on for a number of years, access to that area was forbidden, even to the church.

In such a dramatic situation, the Friends in collaboration with Mennonite Central Committee formed the first peacemakers group. This committee was made up of about 350 people, bringing together women, men, and young adults from rival ethnic groups. It accomplished some remarkable things. First of all, it did what it could to reopen the primary schools. It gathered young persons together into recreational and activity groups such as theater and soccer. It organized work camps to help rebuild various destroyed buildings and infrastructure. It also called for the reopening of secondary schools. And each time there were problems between the rebels and the government, the group did what it could to bring about peace. Because of all of these efforts, the center of Kibimba became a place of refuge instead of a place of chaos.

In addition, the Evangelical Friends tried to establish national and regional committees to promote reconciliation in all of society. In the educational domain, the Friends built Magarama, an elementary school in Gitega focused on peacemaking. The school is still running today and has trained many children in the principles of peace. It continues to accept children from different ethnic backgrounds that in any other situation would be discriminated against.

Today Friends have thirteen schools—eleven primary and two secondary. We are aiming to establish peace education programs in all these schools, patterned after the pioneering work done at Magarama School. Our goal is to get peace education curricula adopted in all Burundi public schools. We are working on elementary teaching materials now and will prepare secondary educational materials next.

In the area of health, we have set up a clinic to provide health education in remote locales where there have been many armed conflicts and where medical care is unavailable. In the area of social services, a group of benefactors has been formed called Abagiraneza to help reconstruct the homes of over 160 families whose homes were destroyed by violence. Various groups have helped the transient population through the distribution of food and clothing. Some have gone to prison and refugee camps. They have also visited refugee camps in Tanzania and established programs to provide psychological help and comfort in anticipation of these people returning to their home countries.

To reach the greatest number of people, the Friends Church has also created a three-month training session for men and women coming from different churches. These people later formed an organization called the Mission for Peace and Reconciliation Under the Cross (MIPAREC), based at Gitega. It is working on such things as establishing community reconciliation and peace committees to manage community conflict. There is another program focused on women and families to help with marital problems and train children. There is still another program for youth addressing juvenile delinquency. There is a peace education program active in secondary schools. There is program whose goal is to produce peace resources. The group also plays a major role in the reconciliation of former combatants with their communities. Yet one more initiative is the establishment of a program for trauma treatment and reconciliation to aid the victims of violence.

In this admirable work, Burundi Friends have not had to toil alone. We have benefited from the help and support of national and international organizations, such as the National Council of Churches in Burundi, CAPP (Change Agent Peace Project), Mennonite Central Committee, and Christian Aid. The legal authorities have begun to reinforce the structures for managing conflict within both the church and the community. The church is working on setting up welcoming committees to respond to the social needs of those recovering through peace initiatives. The church expects to increase its strength to be more effective and active and to become a formidable peace maker at the national level.

In conclusion, Burundi is a country that has been overwhelmed by the ethnic violence that has gripped it for four decades. These conflicts have destroyed the infrastructure and broken the hearts of our citizens. The Evangelical Friends Church, a Historic Peace Church, has been hurt a great deal but has not given up. We have undertaken many projects of which we can be proud, and we are looking to the future with even more confidence in the goal of becoming an effective peace maker in Burundi and the surrounding area.

22

DETRAUMATIZATION IN RWANDA

Cecile Nyiramana (Rwanda)

BECAUSE OF THE UNPRECEDENTED DISASTER we experienced in 1994 in Rwanda, the Evangelical Friends Church in Rwanda was faced with an enormous challenge. We decided do everything we could to help reconstruct relationships. The church itself lost a large number of members who were either killed or went into exile. After the genocide in 1994, the Government of Unity and Reconciliation began to repatriate large numbers of refugees. Keep in mind that two previous times that many people became refugees, in 1959 and 1973. So when an even larger number of people became refugees in 1994, it became quite urgent to begin the resettlement process promptly. But this was easier to say than to do, for everyone was suffering. Some had been wounded and nearly everyone was traumatized.

Friends in Rwanda became actively involved in support of the policies of unity and reconciliation, thanks in part to the help received from other countries. The first step was to organize seminars on conflict management, detraumatization, unity, and reconciliation. We set about to help the many orphans and widows and to aid in the repatriation and reintegration of refugees. We committed ourselves to helping the prisoners morally as well as spiritually. We had to reconstruct the churches which had been destroyed during the events, so regular worship services could resume.

One way we sought to impact the broader society was through forming peace committees and teams of peacemakers in all areas of the country. These groups sponsored peace and reconciliation seminars that proved to be very productive. To bring together Rwandans and help to reconstruct relationships, we have organized public discussions which have brought together people of different categories and have focused on reconciliation in Rwanda.

Because we realized that we needed to start working with children from a very young age to train a new generation that would know how to live in peace, we've begun peace education programs in the schools. We have also established a Friends Peace House, Urugo Rw'Amahoro, meaning "the family of peace." We see it as our task to rebuild the family on a foundation of peace, beginning at home and broadening out to the community and the nation. So today we are impacting a large number of Rwandans and have a fairly large group of peace agents helping us rebuild peace in our country.

Because of the very large number of people arrested on suspicion of involvement in the genocide, the government decided to adapt a traditional judicial system called the Gacaca. Until this step was taken, the court system had only managed to process 6,000 out of more than a hundred thousand persons in jail. At that rate, many would have died in prison before they could have been judged for their crimes. One of the strengths of the Gacaca system is that it is based on the principle of restorative justice. The goal is to help Rwandans discover the truth surrounding the killings to determine how to establish true justice. There is a commitment in this process to follow the principles of tolerance, love, and forgiveness.

Friends have been supporting the Gacaca process, for we believe this is a viable way to deal with the tens of thousands in jail, some of whom are probably guilty and some innocent. We have worked with the training of Gacaca judges, helping them with the process and to focus on reconciliation and truth. We also have provided help to the victims and have assisted those about to be set free. We discovered that the prisoners had nothing, no clothing except the pink uniforms they wear, no shelter, and no jobs. So we realized we needed to do something about these people, not only their physical needs but also their emotional trauma.

For those orphaned in the genocide, the church has tried to help them get into school, which means finding a way for fees to be paid, uniforms bought, and family support given. For the many widows, the first need is usually to deal with their trauma and then their many physical and economic needs. Some were severely wounded and some raped. They all continue to suffer, even as the healing process begins. Some are homeless and others are just barely surviving. It is useless to talk with people about reconciliation when they are still suffering from trauma

As we would expect, AIDS spread quickly in our country after the genocide. As a church we have put a lot of effort into raising people's consciousness of the HIV / AIDS problem without stigmatizing those already infected with this disease. Just as violence has produced orphans and widows, the same has resulted from AIDS, so we are doing our best to take in those who have lost their families.

We are going to continue to work hard at educating youth for peacemaking. The message we are communicating to the young people is "No More Genocide!" We need to promote peace among the youth because they are the strength and the future of our country. We also have to educate the youth to be self-sufficient because there are those who use others to destroy peace.

In these efforts we would like to have as much help as possible from those who are trained in peacemaking and conflict resolution. We would be grateful for help from the other peace churches, for until now we are the only Historic Peace Church working in Rwanda. But we are grateful for the efforts of the Mennonites through the Mennonite Central Committee, who have been helping with the education of women and children as well as training in conflict management. Quakers from other countries have helped us through the American Friends Service Committee and the Africa Great Lakes Initiative.

We ask those who read this to pray for us in our work, for there are many threats to peace. There are so many children who are not in school. Please pray for Rwanda, for peace in Rwanda. We truly need this. And pray as well for our entire region, the Great Lakes area, for there are troubles in every country that borders these lakes. Pray for those who have been hurt by the conflicts, so they can come out of their trauma, so they can accept reconciliation.

23

KERNELS FOR PEACE IN SOUTH KIVU

Ramazani Kakozi (Congo)

THE PEOPLE OF BUKAVU, the major city of South Kivu province, are going through a very difficult time. There is little food and essentially no medicine. Its a population which must rely almost entirely on itself, for the government has made promises that have not materialized. Only a little help has come from United Nations organizations such as the Office for the Coordination of Humanitarian Affairs and the World Food Program. A few non-governmental organizations such as CARITAS, the Catholic relief group, have tried to help, but the needs are greater than the available resources.

As for the Friends Church in eastern Congo, we have had no loss of human life and praise the Eternal One for having spared us. But many of our members have lost all of their possessions to looting. For the time being, they have not gotten much help, but we have had promises of help from certain benefactors and missionary groups.

Our church is still young and we have few internal resources to draw on. The Friends Church came to Congo from nearby Burundi. In 1991 the president of Congo signed a document saying that the church had the right to function throughout the country. For now, we are active in the provinces of North Kivu and South Kivu and have about 4,000 members. We also have an annual conference or yearly meeting, which has been meeting regularly for some time. One of the recent examples of God's blessing on our church was the good news that the wife of our legal representative, Mkoko, gave birth to a girl while the bullets were flying. For us that was another sign of all that God has done for us.

A major issue that has faced our province and our church has been the problem of peaceful coexistence among the ethnic groups in the province. Some of our members are Bamyamulenge, the people whose roots are in Rwanda. After the capture of Bukavu by the loyalist soldiers, all of the Bamyamulenge of Bukavu and of Uvira left the town to take refuge either in Chambugu or in Bujumbura. When an entire ethnic group has to leave an area, their displacement causes tensions even for those who remain, and that's the current situation in South Kivu. The government is doing some things to calm the tensions, but the problem is still with us.

We in the Friends Church have not stood by with our arms crossed. In 1999 when the second crisis broke out, with the support of a Norwegian peace program we began to organize seminars and workshops on peacemaking and conflict resolution for the benefit of our church members. We trained about sixty facilitators and have already begun spreading out into the church districts. In 2001, our yearly meeting created a Department of Peace Education, which I currently direct. This department has an extensive program of peace education, with a number of short-, medium-, and long-term goals. This work is to be carried out by a group called "Agents for the Promotion of Peace." Its projects include peace workshops, Young Peacemakers, peace education programs in the schools of North and South Kivu, Women and Families for Peace, our peace center and guest house under construction, and a trauma clinic under construction.

I want to give particular attention to the project called "Women and Families for Peace." How did we come up with this idea? First we realized that decisions concerning Congo being made at the United Nations and in other international venues have involved our political leaders alone, most of them men. The grassroots population didn't even know what was going on. If I water a plant, only the leaves will feel it. It will take a while for the roots to benefit. Similarly the decisions made in high places don't generally touch the general population. At this moment, lots of Congolese don't know anything about diplomatic agreements like the Lusaka and the Pretoria accords.

But the truth is that all the wars that happen, whether in Congo, Burundi, or Rwanda, greatly affect women and children. So we said to ourselves, Let's take women and children as our starting point for teaching peace, because women get to know each other faster than men. And children get to know each other more quickly than their parents. As soon as a woman has a message of peace, she will communicate it to her neighbors. In this way the message will circulate through the neighborhood or village rather quickly.

So we organized the Women and Families for Peace project, and it is composed of five groups: Kigongo, Abéka, Atungulu, Mienge, and Bukavu. The members are organized in small cells, called Kernels for Peace. Currently we have seventy-eight kernel groups and 2,024 members who have joined this project. It is not sufficient to simply say that you want to be a member, for there's a charter that you must sign to show that you've become a member, and you must agree to the following:

> We, the members of the kernels, circles, and networks of Women and Families for Peace in South Kivu, being activists for peace, committed to the promotion of positive values within our families and our society, have decided as a result of training received concerning peaceful resolution of conflict and peaceful coexistence of local communities, to bestow upon ourselves the present charter:
>
> 1. We promise resolutely to spread the training we have received concerning conflict resolution and peaceful coexistence.
>
> 2. We commit ourselves to the respect for human rights, especially for women and children.
>
> 3. We commit ourselves to the respect for property, whether private or public.
>
> 4. We will maintain the spirit of service while exercising the responsibilities entrusted to us.
>
> 5. We prioritize the peaceful resolution of conflict via dialogue, rejecting recourse to violence in any form.
>
> 6. We will refrain from any form of social discrimination, especially pertaining to sex, race, color, religion, ethnic, or other identity.
>
> 7. We will distance ourselves from any armed group and will do everything possible to discourage and dissuade our family members and associates from joining such groups.
>
> 8. We will refuse to ally ourselves with any political party, movement, or association that proposes to use force, war, or other forms of violence to attain their objectives.

We also have other projects in process. For example, we are constructing a peace center and guest house in Uvira and we have just laid the cornerstone of a trauma clinic. You can understand that in a region so disturbed since 1960, where people have seen all possible types of violence, we must detraumatize many people. At the trauma clinic we've already begun training trauma counselors who will work in various villages.

The success of all these projects requires human, financial, and material resources which our young church currently lacks. This is why we are expressing an appeal to all of you and through you to the churches and charitable organizations in your respective countries, that you might come to our aid so we can achieve the goals articulated for each of these projects.

24

OVERCOMING TRIBALISM IN THE CONGO

Pascal Tshisola Kulungu (Congo)

THIS HISTORY THAT I AM ABOUT TO TELL is one that I personally experienced within the church. Let me remind you that the Republic of Congo has seen its peace threatened in many ways in recent years by war, tribal conflict, interfaith conflict, conflicts within families, and also conflict within institutions. Where does this trouble come from? From the churches, from the peacebuilders, and from those who can intervene with political leaders.

Except for India, Congo has more Mennonites than any other country in the world. We have about 200,000 members organized into three groups. This story comes from one of those groups, the Communaute des Eglises des Freres Mennonite au Congo (CEFMC, the Mennonite Brethren Church in Congo). This church goes all the way back to the 1930s. After the missionaries left, the church was independently governed. With the passage of time, the structure of the church changed. In 1998, the church received new leadership. There were two particular leaders who I am going to talk about, Monsieur Ndunda Ngelego who was the General Secretary and legal representative, and Mukashiyenu Tshimbadi, who was the conference evangelist. These leaders had to deal with the conflicts within the church.

Long ago, the church was administered from one central office in Kikwit with a structure of three regions: the western region was centered in the city of Kinshasa; the northern region was administered out of Kikwit; and the southern region was in the district of Panzi. The leaders realized that they needed a new system, and they proposed one with a central office and six "pools."

The six pools were the cities of Kikwit, Kafumba, Kipungu, Kajiji, Panzi, and Kinshasa. This plan was proposed in a special assembly. At this meeting a number of people were against creation of the system, particularly the people from the cities of Kinshasa and Panzi. But three-quarters of the church members favored establishing the system of the pools. The discussions went on but did not come to a reasonable solution, so the members decided to have another business session a year later. When people came to the next meeting, they met pretty much the same results. In particular those from Kinshasa and Panzi were resisting this new structure composed of pools. And the others were pretty much saying the church needed to change to this system. The discussion ended with the two teams from Kinshasa and Panzi leaving the room in anger.

The ones who remained did decide to implement the new system of pools—and that is the source of this discord within the church. There was no further communication between Kinshasa and Panzi and the central office. There were no visits, no working together, and no communication. Those from Kinshasa basically had their origins in Panzi, so the problem was really tribal as much as anything else. And those of us who wanted to make peace did not have the means to do this. We had the desire but not the means to do it.

So we began to speak with our traditional partners, the MCC (Mennonite Central Committee) and MBMSI (Mennonite Brethren Missions and Service International) and began to ask ourselves, "What can we do?" And we were given $2,000 to help with the resolution. So we organized a team of lawyers, professors, and myself.

We started with meetings with the Kinshasans and decided on pools within the city of Kinshasa. Then we went to Kikwit to do a similar thing, after having had workshops and seminars. We listened a long time to the people at the three major sites—Kinshasa, Kikwit, and Panzi, then we tried hard to discern what elements were causing the conflicts. First of all we decided that the old system of organization was very inefficient in terms of projects. By contrast the system of pools did work rather well. But the people of Kinshasa criticized this approach, saying that the government did not recognize the pools. Documents needed to be in place first. Furthermore, the city of Kinshasa could not function well with a rotational system of leadership.

These experts then decided that the main office of the CEFMC, the Mennonite Brethren Church, would remain in the city of Kikwit and be the main coordinating office. This office would be administered by two people, the legal representative and the community evangelist. The office in Kinshasa would have a special status by itself. Whereas there previously was one coordinator, now there would be three, each in charge of a different area of administration, evangelization, and finance. The station of Panzi would become the center for the southern districts. And these five places would then become pools with each of the areas around them: Kajiji, Kipungu, Tembo, Kikwit, and Kafumba. There is a difference between the pools and the regions, and Kinshasa has a special status that allows us to work out these complex differences between the system of pools and regions.

They named a commission to develop these new statutes and to organize further discussion at the General Assembly. A religious service dedicated to reconciliation was organized in Kinshasa, and it was to unite the delegates, members, and decision-makers of Kinshasa.

Now there are in fact very good relationships between the different groups which had previously been wrapped up in the conflict. In other words, the peace that had formerly been much threatened now is functioning well. This is a good illustration of how conflict can be handled, not only within a civil society but also within the church itself.

On the basis of my personal experience, I offer two concluding thoughts. First, it seems to me that this subject of peaceful resolution of conflict is a question of public health, because we use the term *public health* to talk about all the problems that threaten the well-being of our people. That is why, when we're talking about peacemaking and reconciliation, we need to think about the consequences for public health.

Second, we have people who have not received the message of reconciliation. These are people who are trained in the Bible but nevertheless have created conflict themselves. We need to "convert" them to the message and practice of peace, so they can be constructive members of our Christian community. This is how the Mennonite spirit of reconciliation can help work out problems born within the church itself. The Mennonite church within the Congo is one of those places where discord was able to be solved within the church, and it can be an example for other churches.

TOWARD
PEACE IN SUDAN

Harold Miller (USA)

This material first appeared in the Mennonite Central Committee Peace Office Newsletter, *"Peace and Pain in Sudan," vol. 35, no. 2 (April-June, 2005), pp. 1-5. Used here by permission of the MCC Peace Office. This chapter builds on material introduced in chapter 19 of this book.*

THE ROLE OF THE CHURCH

Although the Sudan is predominantly Muslim, a Christian minority—southern Sudanese plus Coptic (Egyptian) Christians—has become conspicuous in recent decades by speaking out on war and peace and by providing humanitarian services. Already in 1972, the Sudan Council of Churches (SCC) was implementing relief, rehabilitation, and resettlement programs following the Addis Ababa Peace Agreement. Support for this Sudanese church engagement came from an ecumenical network of church-related agencies, including Mennonite Central Committee (MCC). MCC personnel were first seconded to the SCC in 1973, followed by significant numbers of personnel and other forms of support. MCC's relationships with the SCC and later with the New Sudan Council of Churches in the south have been sustained to this day.

The entry of the Sudanese churches into the public arena has stimulated many auxiliary interests and activities, including a revisiting of

Sudan's Christian antecedents, recorded in considerable detail in the Faith in Sudan book series (see Roland Werner in *Day of Devastation, Day of Contentment*, Nairobi: Paulines, 2001, pp. 21-120). Sudan's ancient (Nubian) church (500–1500 A.D.) traces its beginnings to early missionary outreach from the Coptic Church and the ancient Church of Constantinople. The first African Christian reported in the Bible was the Ethiopian eunuch mentioned in Acts chapter 8, a person who lived in what is today north Sudan. Today Sudanese Christians are bold to claim Nubian Christianity as part of their faith heritage and as part of Sudan's officially acknowledged history.

Modern Christianity came to Sudan in the mid-1800s championed by the illustrious Italian Catholic missionary leader, Daniel Comboni. Anglicans entered Sudan at the formation of the Condominium government, followed by Presbyterians. Coptic and Armenian Christians have long been present though now in declining numbers.

By 1983, a second phase of the civil war in south Sudan had reignited, isolating SCC services in government-controlled areas. In response, the churches of Sudan agreed in 1990 to establish a second Christian Council—the New Sudan Council of Churches (NSCC)—to serve member churches in rebel-controlled south Sudan. Church leaders have affirmed the two councils as an expression of a common ecumenical reality.

Since the 1990s, the two Christian councils have increasingly collaborated under the ecumenical framework of the Sudan Ecumenical Forum (SEF), comprising churches from Sudan and the international ecumenical support community. Meeting about every eighteen months, the SEF helped to sustain common Christian purpose in Sudan during the civil war. It also sponsored high-profile consultations convened by the two Christian councils to address issues of war and peace. Emanating from these deliberations came statements and initiatives widely publicized to all levels of Sudanese society and beyond.

SUDAN'S TRANSFORMATION

Sudan is grappling with the complexities of war and peace. If transition periods in other African crisis situations serve as precedents, transition time is testing time for government, for church, and for all civil society agencies working for the shift from a highly conflicted to a more peaceful body politic. Sudan has been radically transformed by both its war and reconstruction experiences.

Not since the height of the slave trade in the 1800s have so many southern Sudanese been present in north Sudan. Nearly half of the population of Khartoum is southern Sudanese. All major towns throughout northern Sudan now feature significant numbers of southerners. Along with this shift of people, the Christian church has become more visible in the north.

Years ago, a tattered, soiled poster graced the entrance to Khartoum's National Museum featuring, as memory recalls, the following words: "Sudan, the country with a glorious past!" Today, visions for the future of Sudan are challenging and various.

For the government of Sudan (GoS), the paramount goal in this transition time is to maintain political and economic power. For rebel politicians such as John Garang, the challenge is to include all of Sudan's marginalized peoples toward the elusive goal of national unity. For rank and file southerners, deep feelings of fear and distrust remain. For many the goal is separation or some degree of autonomy. The southerners exiled in neighboring countries want to return to south Sudan, but only after peace and stability are assured. For rebels in Darfur and other marginalized areas, the aspiration is for full participation in the political and economic fortunes of the country.

Further afield, the options for Sudan are being shaped by a kaleidoscope of dynamics. From the United States there has been pressure for a timely conclusion to the peace negotiations. The U.S. is also concerned that Sudan be weaned from its empathy for fundamentalist Islam. Sudan's tantalizing oil reserves are controlled and exploited by China, Malaysia, and India, just beyond easy reach of the West. With regard to Darfur, the U.S. government has used the word *genocide* but has not implemented the sanctions associated with the use of that term.

As a bridge between Africa and the Middle East, Sudan has long managed divided loyalties. The GoS has maintained close ties with the Arab League and has thus been beholden to the political and religious dynamics of the Middle East. The cauldron that is Iraq and the unresolved Israeli-Palestinian problem ensure that the Middle East agenda retains priority status. Meanwhile, the demise of apartheid in South Africa in the early 1990s and the "African Renaissance" constitute dynamics that are also not easily ignored. The GoS has done its best to be on good terms with both Middle Eastern and African political demands.

The distinctly African nature of the Inter-Governmental Authority for Development peace negotiations has ensured—contrary to earlier GoS insistence—that war and peace in Sudan functions as an African concern. In the case of Darfur, the GoS has negotiated with rebel groups under the African Union, initially to arrange a cease-fire, but possibly working in the longer term toward power sharing on the model of the peace agreement signed between the GoS and the SPLM/A.

SOMETHING NEW

In the Horn of Africa region over the past several years, two predominantly Muslim African states—Sudan and Somalia—subjected their respective conflicts to mediation/resolution by African institutions (IGAD) and African mediator personalities. Today, many would agree with Pliny the Elder, the ancient Africanist observer, when he exclaimed, *"Ex Afrika semper aliquid novum"* ("Out of Africa, there is always something new!"). Indeed, there is new momentum underway in Africa; these negotiations followed the larger cross-continental pattern in which African mediators and processes—enjoying growing strength and trust—have been resolving African conflicts.

Within the faith community, similar precedents are being established. During the 1997 general assembly of the AACC, the Archbishop Desmond Tutu Peace Prize was awarded to two representatives—one Christian and one Muslim—of the Inter-Faith Council of Liberia for mediating and resolving conflict between contending Liberian political dynamics. Meanwhile, at the level of the AACC there is encouragement to establish Inter-Faith Councils in African countries with significant Muslim and Christian populations. While they may not function perfectly or conclusively, they can be recognized and appreciated as an African response to an African situation. Today Africa is far from stable, but institutional patterns and general expectations suggest some positive directions. Appreciation of these dynamics provides perspective through which to express solidarity with the people of Sudan and the people of the African continent.

26

CARING FOR VICTIMS IN KENYA

Nora Musundi (Kenya)

WHEN I WAS A LITTLE GIRL, I used to listen to my grandmother, who was a wonderful storyteller. She used to sing many songs to us as well. My mother was a devout Christian who believed in the Lord and was a very peaceful person. She was kind, humble, generous, and loving. She used to pray when things seemed impossible and she set a good example to her family and church members. She was very generous. Our relatives used to come to our place for meals, and she would always provide for them.

Before I got married I prayed that God would give me a man who would give me peace, and I'm glad that prayer was answered, for my husband is a man of peace. He supports me in whatever I do. Even our children do the same. Everything comes from family. My mother taught me that to have peace is to have a good relationship with God and with other people. The goal is to try and understand other people and accept them as they are, so that you can pray and help them to become what God wants. We find many biblical references to support this point, such as Leviticus 26:6, Romans 5:1, Matthew 5:9, and John 14:27.

When Jesus started his ministry, he presented a great message to his disciples and the other people who listened to him which we call the Sermon on the Mount. Matthew 5:9 says, "Blessed are the peacemakers, for they will be called children of God." And also when he was leaving, he said to his disciples in John 14:27, "Peace I leave with you, my peace I give to you. I do not give as the world gives." This is special to a people who are ready to listen, obey, and care for others.

In Kenya, all the Friends people used to be in one yearly meeting, started in 1946. People acted together. But a time came when people did not trust one another. It was difficult to get along. A group decided to break away from the yearly meeting. When they did, other groups followed. Where there had been peace, we now had conflict. As this situation went on, women in my village decided to form a prayer group. This prayer group used to go to families to pray with them, and occasionally we would take food to these families. This was a rewarding ministry, but it was sad to hear some of the stories told by these families. I don't know about other countries, but in Kenya you will find families who are peaceful but others that quarrel. In Kenya we don't have divorce, but we have separation and frequently family conflict.

Our prayer group used to go to quiet places along the river banks to listen to the birds singing and to look at the different trees. Seeing the wonderful things that God made was a way to bring peace to troubled people. On Easter morning in 1989, we went to a beautiful river early in the morning and decided that every woman should find her own spot, sit there, look at the trees and the hills, listen to the birds singing, and then look at the water. This river had five streams. Where these five streams came together there was a home. Can you picture it? The water comes together with great force and then becomes quiet again. I think you all have seen waterfalls. After watching this waterfall we had hope that our problems were going to be solved and that God is who knows how to solve such problems. From that waterfall we learned a lot of things.

In 1991, after the Friends World Committee for Consultation met in Kenya, the Friends women came together and decided to form a prayer group for women from all of Kenya. It was very wonderful for me to see these women coming together to pray. I praised the Lord because I saw in that coming together the meaning of the waterfall. When these women decided to gather for prayer, they decided to meet quarterly, going from one yearly meeting to another. That is my prayer group—a national prayer group in which I am a pastor. I praise God for the healing brought about by the women, because women realized that we needed peace in our families, in our churches, and in our country.

In 1991 Kenya experienced an outbreak of ethnic clashes in many parts of the country. The violence included the burning of houses and the killing of many innocent people. It was very difficult. These clashes were politically motivated and supported by the government in place at the time. I saw mothers coming, their babies on their backs, walking along with small children, carrying a few items which would be useful where they settled. These women and children walked long distances to find water, food, and other necessities. When I saw this I told my husband, and he was concerned too. We went to our ancestral home and found that some people had taken shelter in our house, where we don't live any longer. We prayed with these displaced families and then returned, feeling very sorry for these families.

When we returned home, we continued to feel the burden to feed those who had been displaced by the violence. We had some beans and maize, bananas, and other things, which we felt we should use to feed these displaced families. Later, when we began to run out of food, we asked some friends at church to help. We formed a distress committee and from the Africa section of the Friends World Committee for Consultation we received food, clothes, and money. We worked hard to provide help to those in need, but there was not enough for everyone.

In 1992 I was blessed to be able to attend a peace conference in Zimbabwe organized by African women. The organizers called themselves "Peace Creators." One speaker was the wife of the president of Zimbabwe. She said she did not enjoy the privilege of being the wife of the president while children and women were suffering because of the effects of war. We were sad when we heard some of the stories from our Zimbabwean friends. This woman challenged us when we got back to our countries to make peace in our own small ways. It is sinful not to do what is right when you know what to do. I was really challenged, because I had been criticized by some people who said that I was feeding people because I had a car, because I had food, and because I had money.

I was discouraged as a result of these negative comments. But when I came home from the conference I was ready to set about feeding the displaced families once again.

This time our feeding efforts concentrated on our ancestral home, where so many families needed shelter and food. During this time my husband and I decided to give an acre of land to this community, so they could build a dispensary. The children of these families were suffering from malaria, pneumonia, and other diseases. So these people worked hard and built a nice dispensary. If you go there today, you will find people from three tribes coming together as one community to get health care from this dispensary. I thank God, for this has been the most successful such project in western Kenya.

In 1993 I joined a committee of the National Council of Churches in Kenya to go around the country and try to find out what caused the clashes and to encourage people who were suffering. When we went around, we met church leaders, counselors, village elders, house-wives, and others. As we talked to them, we discovered that many did not know the cause of the clashes. But people were willing to work to-gether for peace, and the youth promised to cooperate. By the time we concluded the work of this task force, some people had gone back to their original homes, but others found it difficult to go back. They had to exchange their pieces of land with the majority people from the area where they came from. And others bought plots near the markets and in towns, where they would be safe.

These ethnic clashes helped awaken Kenyans to the dangers of tribal hatred. We will never be the same. In the past the people of these tribes would interact with one another and tribal members would sometimes intermarry. They would do things together. But now after the land clashes, they wouldn't. Because now people knew, "I'm this particular tribe, and he's this tribe." So they were no longer comfort-able being together.

By 1997 our Friends prayer group had grown in numbers. Some-times we prayed throughout the night for peace and unity for our churches and our country as a whole. We prayed for families, because people had started dying from HIV/AIDS, and we saw these children suffering. We decided we needed to do something to help. People did little things like selling eggs, chickens, and bananas to get enough to buy a plot, and on this plot we built a semi-permanent structure for the AIDS project.

Before the 2002 elections, we fasted and prayed that God would help Kenya have peace during the elections. We thank God for an-swering our prayers and providing peace during this critical election. President Moi stepped aside gracefully to make way for a new begin-ning and government. Once again we were reminded of the water-falls, because these people of different political parties began to think about coming together to form one party and they eventually did.

Our prayer group decided to write a proposal for a project to take care of HIV victims and orphans, because there were so many or-phans. We also proposed that we provide training for school dropouts in tailoring and carpentry, so they would be ready to face the future. In answer to our prayers, we received a grant from an organization in the United States, the Right Sharing of World Resources that enabled us to start the classes.

We also sought funding for a center for guiding and counseling those in need of peace and prayer in their families and in their churches. After we built the center, we were praying and became concerned about the orphans. If you went to their home, you would find the children by themselves, for the parents were dead. The children were there without food, and their relatives came and looted the property which remained. So we started feeding these children.

Once again God honored our faithfulness and we received a grant from UNICEF for this very purpose. We were very happy. The women sang in praise to God for having opened the ways to help them to feed these children. And after we got the grant we were given additional funds for buying uniforms and paying school fees for some of the children.

The strength behind our work is always prayer. When we come together in that small building of ours, we pray, we do Bible study, and we sing. One of the songs the women sing is, "God, you are the God of miracles. I just wonder how you are." And this song gives them courage because they know God is a God of miracles. Our prayer group hopes that God will bring even more women who are willing to help continue this service, especially at this time when Kenya is facing a very difficult period, politically and economically. There is a drought in many parts of the country now.

While we have been working on providing peace and compassion to the people in need, we have seen some answers to prayer in the healing of conflict in the Friends Church in Kenya. We have experienced much discord, but we are pleased that all Quakers today in Kenya are united under the umbrella of the Friends Council of Kenya. In 2001, all the yearly meetings held a reconciliation meeting in which the people were willing to forgive one another and to commit to work together in harmony. The people expressed regret for the years of quarreling, misunderstanding, and mistrust. They realized that the time had come to work together.

Forgiveness is very, crucial. If we forgive one another, that is when we can understand each other and work together. To understand is to stand under somebody's problems, which is not easy. We women stand under our husbands' problems. But it is not easy. With prayer, we can manage it.

So the thing that I want you to know is that when we come together in the blood of Jesus and forgive one another, we can work together for peace. I want to leave you with a challenge. The reader can start peacemaking in some small way like we did. My prayer group has done its peacemaking in small ways, yet we have accomplished quite a lot. When we all join together in prayer for one another, we find fruitful avenues of peacemaking wherever we are.

A Living Peace Theology
Dean Johnson (USA)

It's fascinating to me to hear from our African brothers and sisters a really lived peace church theology. So often we in North America talk about what it means to be a peace church. But when it comes to actually confronting the powers and principalities, we do little. What do you say to a group of people facing violence in their lives every day? That's the real question in Africa. How far does tolerance stretch? How far can tolerance go? In many cases these are really hopeless situations, and the power of the human spirit, the power of the community, seems to keep the community driving forward, striving for a real sense of peace.

I've heard stories about how people have befriended their Muslim neighbors in times of need, which helps build bridges between those two communities, especially in Nigeria where there are many tensions. I've also heard about people who have been abused just walking down the street or coming to the airport. As Christians they were abused by Muslims. Hopefully as they come together to talk about how they've met those challenges in their own communities, they are giving a sense of hope to their brothers and sisters who listen to them.

I think the peace churches have to make a difference and have to embody a living peace theology to be a further example for others. Christianity isn't just about doctrine and the proclamation of accepting Jesus as your Lord and Savior. It really embodies an ethic. It embodies a theology that is alive, that interacts with the culture around it and responds actively to the things that are happening, especially to the violence that is happening. Jesus is the Prince of Peace, and a sound biblical theology backs that up. These folks in the Historic Peace Churches in Africa are really an embodiment of what a living peace theology looks like.

PART V

STORIES OF PEACEMAKING IN THE PUBLIC SQUARE

*Stories of how the Historic Peace Churches
have responded to violence in the public arena*

27

CHRISTIAN FAITHFULNESS AND THE COMMON GOOD

Toma A. Ragnjiya (Nigeria)

CHRISTIAN-MUSLIM RELATIONS IN NIGERIA

I was born between African traditional religion and Islam but now I am a Christian pastor of Ekklesiyar Yan'uwa a Nigeria (the EYN, the Church of the Brethren in Nigeria). We live out the African philosophy and worldview propounded by John S. Mbiti, "I am because we are; since we are, therefore I am." In the Christian context this is comparable to "So in Christ we who are many form one body, and each member belongs to all the others" (Rom. 12:5, NIV). What does this mean to me as a Christian today? Can the Nigerian Christian community maintain faithfulness to the mission of Christ's peace and contribute to the common good in the Nigeria of our time?

The theme of peace theology in Africa is indeed a challenge but most importantly an invitation to reexamine our ministry in the name of Christ . What is this ministry and how do we realize it? I believe the ministry entrusted to us by the Lord is to be faithful to the Father. Faithfulness that requires love is a key to all relationships, and with right relationship comes peace, shalom.

When thinking of peace theology in Africa, we should be aware that theology is something one cannot learn by reading textbooks or listening to lectures but by engaging in doing theology in particular contexts and situations. In this case we will consider the Nigerian context. Doing theology in this way will help us to be more insightful and more faithful to the gospel. We have to learn how to minister in ways that relate to the wider needs of the society.

My intention in this chapter is to give an overview of the relationship between Christians and Muslims and to discuss how religion has been dragged into politics and vice-versa. I will then suggest ways by which these two major religions can contribute to the common good and to peace. I will also draw on resources for peace from the two religious traditions and recommend some ways to address tensions between them.

We assume that theology throughout Africa finds its common ground in three basic elements: in the Bible and Christian tradition, in African culture and religion, and in the contemporary socio-political situation. These three elements vary in intensity according to the situation in which African theologians or church leaders find themselves. While all three elements have their place in the Nigerian situation, the contemporary socio-political situation is relevant as a source of conflict in the country. I assume all of us are aware that theology becomes a sterile exercise if it fails to deal with contemporary factors.

The most populous country in Africa, Nigeria, has over 120 million people and an equal percentage of Christians and Muslims. It is a multicultural and multi-religious society that has lived together harmoniously for many years. However, the situation changed with the introduction of the Islamic Sharia law in 1999. When the state government of Kaduna expressed the intent to introduce the law, the event sparked serious violence.

Although Zamfara was the first state to introduce the "law" fully after the Kaduna crisis, no violence took place out there. The absence of violence may be attributed to the fact that the population in Zamfara is over 90 ninety percent Muslim. But this wasn't the case in Kaduna, which has a mixture of religious followers. Kaduna has also been called the "no-man's land" of Nigeria. The introduction of Sharia in Kaduna met with violent reaction among non-Muslim residents. This incident left about 1,000 people dead and an estimated 80,000 displaced from their homes. Homes were destroyed and businesses looted, threatening harmony and peace across the country. The relationship between Muslims and Christians reached its lowest ebb.

The violent situation became a concern for both Muslim and Christian leaders. They started exploring ways of restoring trust and harmony through the Christian Association of Nigeria and the Islamic Supreme Council of Nigeria. Several initiatives were undertaken, one of which was to persuade two religious leaders, a pastor and an imam who had been responsible for preaching hatred and war against each other, to become collaborators for dialogue and peace. For a number of years Nigeria was known for its religious tolerance. Every faith was accorded its due. Muslims respected the sanctity of the churches, Christians respected the sanctity of the mosques, and both faiths respected the traditional religions or worshipers of "shrines."

However, today Nigeria is known the world over for its inter-religious tensions and conflicts that hinder peaceful coexistence and harmony. Religion has become a tool of politics and provides a convenient dividing line between populations that differ ethnically, culturally, geographically, and economically. At the root of the tension is the competition for jobs, patronage, and control of the government at local, state, and federal levels. The role of the media is also crucial as local conflicts get transformed into national issues by media coverage. This is especially true when the coverage is biased and provocative, as it often is.

THE INFLUENCE OF RELIGION IN POLITICS

I will now examine the political parties that were formed on the basis of religion, ethnicity, and identity. Four major political parties contested for various political offices in May 1999. The Nigerian Peoples Party (NPP) is predominantly composed of people from the north, mostly Muslims, with a few Igbo Christians from the south as allies. At the end of the general elections in 1999, all of the seven states in which this party won were in the north and all the state governors were Muslims. The presidential candidate for the party in the 2003 general election was a strong Muslim and a former military head of state from the north. He picked an Igbo Christian from the south as his running mate.

The Advance for Democracy (AD) party is the most ethnically based because the results of the 1999 elections showed that all the state governors came from the same ethnic group in the west. This party grew out of a strong Yoruba cultural group called "Afenefere."

The All Progressive Grand Alliance (APGA) is an interesting party because Odemegu Ojuku, the former secessionist leader in the civil war, was the presidential candidate .The majority of the party members are easterners from one major ethnic group (Igbo). In one of his campaign speeches, Ojuku said he was running for president not to rule Nigeria but to close the division that dates back to 1914, when the British colonialists fused the northern and southern halves of Nigeria into one country. According to Ojuku, the civil war fought 1967-1970 was actually the result of the horrific power struggle between the south and the north. In another speech he appealed to Nigerians by saying that he did not seek to rule but to heal the Nigerians' troubled polity. Ojuku, educated at Oxford University in England, spoke in the Igbo language in his campaigns to strengthen his ethnic identity.

The People's Democratic Party (PDP), the ruling party, is ethnically mixed and has the most influential people of Nigeria. The PDP has control of twenty-eight of the thirty-six states of Nigeria. If one reads Nigerian newspapers from the political campaign periods of 1999, one finds that most newspapers identify president Obasanjo and Bukhara (NPP presidential candidate) less in terms of political positions than their origins and ways of life. Obasanjo is a Christian (Baptist) from the south and General Buhari is a strong Muslim from the north.

The Sharia law has been used as a form of identity and greatly influences Nigerian politics. It is difficult to understand the introduction of Sharia in the northern states in this period. In the past Nigeria had both civilian and military heads of states who were staunch Muslims. For example, Generals Babangida, Buhari, Abacha, and Abdul Salam were all Muslim military leaders, but none introduced Sharia. Yet once a Christian was president of the country, Sharia was introduced. Many Nigerians think the introduction of Sharia in the northern states was to counterbalance the power shift to the south. Some Nigerians think the Muslims were disappointed that Obasanjo appointed many people who did not vote for him but who were of the same ethnic group, thereby bringing many of his ethnic group into power.

Journalist Henko Eso described the Nigerian situation well when he said, "Just as soccer is singularly the sole and the most unifying factor in Nigeria, nothing is as divisive as religion." Things need to change toward a more peaceful coexistence. I personally can remember clearly that during my primary school years things were not like this. I attended a Muslim school with few Christians. We went to school on Sundays, but the Christian students were allowed to go to church for worship each Sunday. In my secondary school we had twenty-five Muslims out of four hundred students. The Muslim students were never threatened, and we respected each other. For example, during the Ramadan (fasting) period, Muslim students were treated with respect. We trusted one another and valued each other's friendship. It is different today.

It is agreed that religion is important in the life of every nation, regardless of their faith or denomination, because religion, when truly practiced in its purest form and spirit, is helpful in the life of our nation. Religion should play a vital role in things like purposeful leadership, community building, social justice, law and order, peacemaking, reconciliation, forgiveness, and the healing of wounds in the community. I would say, and many Nigerians would agree, that no religion in Nigeria or anywhere else should be deemed superior or subordinate to the other. We must be willing to overcome the temptation to mix religion and politics or make religion a tool for politics.

During the several conflicts between Muslims and Christians in northern Nigeria over the years (1984-2002), I observed and experienced how high tensions can rise. Making peace, I believe, requires not only a change of deeds but also a change of heart. Peacemakers must do more than just identify where the cycle of violence may be broken. They must also help those involved in conflict to break out of that cycle and create entirely new relationships. How can Christians and Muslims contribute to the common good if they do not trust each other?

We must find a forum for building trust. We need to return to moral values that embody systems of meaning for both religious groups. In a well-organized workshop, a few selected religious leaders could be encouraged to engage in exercises meaningful to all of them. For example, a few of the participants could talk about painful experiences from the religious conflicts in their lives. I believe sharing such stories can generate common bonds between the two groups as both have experienced the terrible effects of violence. I believe it can be done, because in Nigeria people feel free to talk about spiritual matters anywhere. No wonder Nigeria is considered to be the most religious country in the world . But that does not mean that Nigerians practice their faith more than the rest of the world.

Many values could be discussed, but let me illustrate the point with two other important values: empathy and the sanctity of life. I have personally been asked, along with a Muslim leader, to open community and even political meetings with Christian prayers. We could relate to God's empathy easily. It is common to hear Nigerians across the religions say things like *ikon Allah sai addua*, which literally means, "The power of God is experienced in prayers." Allah is referred to as "the compassionate and the merciful" in the Koran, and Jesus' empathy with others in their suffering is well illustrated in the New Testament.

This could be a way of calling on God to help religious leaders understand and to be involved in an engaging dialogue. Similar discussions can be started on the sanctity of life, a core value in Christian society and one shared across many cultures. Listening to the debate on abortion in America shows us how concerned people are about the sanctity of life, and Nigerian religious leaders would surely be interested in a deep discussion about it.

THE CHALLENGE FOR PEACE THEOLOGY TODAY

What can the church do to maintain her faithfulness to Jesus Christ in the difficult situation of violence and counter-violence in Nigeria? While the church has tried to avoid violence and has never deliberately started conflicts, the church's response to conflict has often been violent and destructive. It has been a great temptation for some of our Christians to embark on what has been called "just war." But what is just in war, even if you are wrongly provoked? Does war restore balance? According to the tradition of the Acholi people in northern Uganda, "Death is not paid for by death, but with life." What did Christ do? Peter thought they were wrongly arresting Jesus and so wanted to "protect" his master. "Then one of them struck the slave of the high priest and cut off his right ear. But Jesus said, 'No more of this!' And he touched the servant's ear and healed him" (Luke 22:50-51).

I can remember a respected elder in the community who told me "Toma, make sure when Muslims burn two churches you burn four mosques." Such words coming from an elder in an African society carries lots of meaning for the youths. It is clear that both Christians and Muslims need further and deeper education on some important concepts in Islam and Christianity.

There is the need to educate Muslims about the two concepts of Jihad. The first meaning of Jihad—*Al-jihad al-akbar*—is inner struggle with ones own personal darkness, and it is the greater Jihad. *Al-jihad al-asghar* means outer struggle with the darkness (social ills in the world). To share their understandings of these important concepts, experienced Muslim scholars and leaders should be requested to have workshops and seminars on these concepts with groups of Muslims and also jointly with Christians. Christians need a deeper understanding of the myths of just war theory, which many Christians think is a New Testament teaching.

RESPONDING TO THE CHALLENGE

How do we as ambassadors of Christ respond to these challenges faithfully? We look to him, our Master, Teacher, King, and Counselor. Christ knew that his was not the kingdom of this world, so he prepared the people who later handed over the mission to us. We must, therefore, keep this light alive with the strength it deserves.

The church in Nigeria can learn from the Mozambique church experience. Hezekia Assifa and George Wachira in their book, *Peace Making and Democratization in Africa*, showed clearly how the church's involvement in negotiations to end the civil war contributed toward peace and justice in their country. The Mozambique church developed some peace activities that could be used by any church that finds herself in conflict and violent situations like those in Nigeria. They had well-organized prayers of intercession every month by all churches in the country. They developed Bible study guides on peace entitled "Called to Peace," and distributed them to all churches. They destroyed children's violent toys, provided relief materials to the hungry, and had effective ministries to refugees. The Nigerian church through the Christian Association of Nigeria (CAN), which is well-organized at all levels of the Nigerian community, could incorporate such ideas into the peace activities they already have and develop a theology of peace in the context of African faith.

Faith, I believe, is the starting point of theology. This becomes crucial as some theologians in the West have been accusing Africa of practicing Christianity without theology. While the accusation may not be totally right, it is also not totally wrong. This could be due to the fact that Africans emphasize the practice of faith rather than theology. We need to have a theology that encounters Jesus, the Prince of Peace. We need a theology of love and commitment to others, obedience to the Word of God, and an understanding of the meaning of God's Word in service. We need a deeper understanding of the meaning of "love your enemy" in our daily lives, the word of God expressed in our daily relationships with our neighbors.

We are aware that our faith is in daily tension with our society. I suggest that the church in Africa institutionalize peace and peacebuilding in our ministry—starting within our individual selves and reaching out to our families, local communities, churches, country, and our continent, Africa. Surely what we see today in Africa is bad news, requiring an appropriate response of the good news of Christ, the good news of love and peace. "Peace I leave with you; my peace I give to you" (John. 14:27). Our being in Christ therefore informs our responses to injustice, conflict and violence in the world.

RESOURCES FOR PEACE FOR
THE PROMOTION OF THE COMMON GOOD

The purpose of examining peace in Islam and Christianity is to establish the spirit of tolerance and peace by exploring the traditional strengths of these religions. It should also be stated that there is no intention of depicting an ideal Islam and Christianity or ignoring controversial matters. That would not serve Christian-Muslim dialogue. If the peace traditions within these religions are emphasized, it is to establish the basis by which Christians and Muslims can live in peaceful coexistence rather than rage.

The questions that need to be answered are these: What are the basic principles and positions of Islam and Christianity in the areas of peace, humanity, justice, tolerance, and coexistence? What are the themes from these traditions that could be drawn upon as resources for peacemaking?

RESOURCES FROM MUSLIM TRADITIONS

Unity in diversity and practical religious pluralism demands tolerance. This tolerance can easily be seen in Muhammad's message and in his behavior toward the "people of the book." The Koran contains a number of passages that confirm this. Thus we find in Koran 2:62 that "those who believe (in the Koran), and those who follow the Jewish (Scriptures), the Christians, the Sabians, and any who believe in God and the last day and work for righteousness, shall have their reward from their Lord: They shall not fear, nor shall they grieve."

Tolerance toward members of other faiths is an essential precondition for people to live in peace and for there to be peace between nations, since tolerance and peace are closely connected. The key to Islamic tolerance is the basic principle of the Koran that there should be no compulsion in religion (Koran 2:256) and that it ultimately depends on God who accepts the (rightful!) faith (Islam) and who does not (Koran 10:99; 3:20). Affirming this position, Daniel L. Smith-Christopher says:

> People came into Islam by choice and not by force. Contrary to lingering medieval propaganda, conversion by force is and always has been rigorously prohibited by Islam. People made the decision to convert not only because of the positive impression they received of the carriers of the message, but also probably because they saw Islam as the wave of the future. (*Subverting Hatred: The Challenge of Nonviolence in Religious Traditions*, New York, Orbis Books, 1998, p. 98)

The prophet Muhammad knew how to use the instrument of tolerance with great skill, not ruling out conflicts, but always being well prepared for them (Koran 2:190-192). He preferred, however, the peaceful regulation of conflicts and always considered the peaceful resolution of enmity and conflict through Allah's help. In this regard, one reads in the Koran, "It may be that God will grant love (and friendship) between you and those whom ye (now) hold as enemies" (Koran 60:7) But if the enemy incline toward peace, do thou (also) incline toward peace and trust in God" (Koran 8:61).

A unique example of Mohammed's diplomacy and basic attitude toward securing peace is the slogan, "the reconciliation of hearts," which he issued at the capture of Mecca in 630 C.E. (Koran 9:60). By this he won over friends among his former enemies, made possible the peaceful building up of the Islamic community, and removed the desire for revenge.

In Koran 2:190, we read, "Fight in the cause of God those who fight you, but do not transgress limits." This means that one should not be the first to wage war, nor should one be the attacker on the offensive. The primary meaning of Jihad is not a war with weapons, but a commitment to the things of Allah and Islam. "And shine in his cause as ye ought to shine" (Koran 22:78). However, the "unbelievers" often reacted to the attempt to win them for Islam with hostility (Koran 22:72, 2:27).

In today's world, peace should be the normal state of affairs in relations between people and communities, not just the final condition after the victory of Islam, which is very unlikely. In our time, peace and peaceful coexistence must be the norm and the goal of all politics. In this age, there should be no possibility of or justification for a just violence/war. Many others working toward peace and stability could multiply these examples cited in the Koran.

RESOURCES FROM CHRISTIAN TRADITIONS

Anyone who studies the New Testament will find there a most urgent call to firm kindness, firm compassion without weakness, firm forgiveness, and firm love for others. The gospel makes no qualifications on this subject. Why should we base our position only on the New Testament? Has the Old Testament nothing to tell us about the love for our neighbor? Surely it has. Jesus came not to inaugurate a new system but to confirm the Old Covenant (Matt. 5:17-20).

He summed up the law of the kingdom of God "which is come near unto you" (Luke 10:9 KJV here and below) in the summary of the law (Matt. 5:21-48), which is certainly taken from the Old Testament. However, he gave these two precepts, law and kingdom, a meaning and scope which were completely new (Matt. 5:17). It is in him that the believers will be able to love God with all their heart, because "the Son of man is come to seek and to save that which was lost" (Luke 19:10); because he "came not to be ministered unto, but to minister, and to give his life as ransom for many" (Mark 10:45); and because his blood of the New Covenant has been poured out (Luke 22:20) for our reconciliation (Eph. 2:14-16).

In fact, love of one's neighbor, which is the law and witness of the redeemed of Christ (John 13:35), takes on a new value through his person as believers are united with him by a living faith (John 15). This is why he can declare so strongly, "A new commandment I give unto you, that you love one another" (John 3:34). It is why he can proclaim with authority, "Ye have heard that it was said to them of old time, 'Thou shall not kill.' But I say unto you that whosoever is angry with his brother is guilty of murder" (Matt. 5:21). "Ye have heard that it was said, 'Thou shall love thy neighbor and hate thine enemy.' But I say unto you, love your enemies (Matt. 5:43).

According to the gospel, to love one's neighbor is also and more particularly to love one's enemies. We should know this already from the parable of the Good Samaritan (Luke 10:25-37). Jesus expressly commands us to "Love your enemies, bless them that curse you, pray for them that persecute you" (Matt. 5:44; Luke 6:27-28; Rom. 12:14). "For if ye love them that love you, what do ye more than others?" (Matt. 5:45-48; Luke 6:31-36). When evil men do grave harm to us by word or deed, over and over again Jesus asks us to forgive them (Matt. 6:14-15; 18:15-35; Mark 11:25). "Ye have heard that it was said; an eye for an eye and a tooth for a tooth; but I say unto you, resist not him that is evil" (Matt. 5:38-42). "Behold," says Jesus, "I send you forth as sheep amid wolves" (Matt.10: 16). For there are certainly wolves, but the sheep of the Good Shepherd must count on only the Good Shepherd to give the wolves what they deserve (Rom. 12:19-20; 16:20); for retribution depends on him alone (Col. 3:23-25; James 5:9). As for the Christians, they must persevere in the path of peace and goodness (Rom. 12:19-20; 1 Pet. 4:12-10; 2 Pet. 2:18-25).

Remarkably, in the New Testament it is never a question of "defending oneself from one's enemies by one's own strength or with arms." Defense is never used except to designate Christians' verbal defense before a tribunal (Luke 12:11; 21:15; Acts 22:1; 24:10). It is surely disturbing to find that this idea of self-defense, the basis of the traditional militarist doctrine, has no biblical support, and that the expression itself does not appear a single time in the New Testament. (G. Tapkida, "Religious Conflict in Jos North Local Government Council," thesis, ECWA Theological Seminary, Jos, Nigeria, 1997.)

It may seem that the foregoing discussion assumes or takes for granted the existence of violent languages and activities in Christian and Muslim traditions. By no means! Scott Appleby calms our anxiety when he says that

> Most religious societies, in fact, have interpreted their experiences of the sacred in such a way as to give religion a paradoxical role in human affairs as the bearer of peace and sword. These apparently contradictory orientations reflect a continuing struggle within religions and within the heart of each believer over the meaning and character of the power encountered in the sacred and its relationship to coercive force or violence. (R. Scott Appleby, *The Ambivalence of the Sacred,* New York, Rowan and Littlefield, 2000, p. 27)

This means that we cannot any longer afford to ignore or deny the violent areas of our traditions. Instead, we must approach them with humility and a willingness to transform them to peacemaking themes. Johnston and Sampson support this approach when they stress that

> If religious communities are to realize their potential for peacemaking, they will need to re-examine their primary language self-critically . . . to search their scriptural doctrinal foundations and their own histories to discover the motivation, guidance, and resources for making peace. Religious communities will have to take a long, hard look at themselves and, when appropriate, admit that not everything said in their tradition points in the direction of peace, but actually some produces strife. . . . The

challenge for religious people committed to making peace, then, is to disentangle the themes of conflict in their traditions from the themes of peace and to employ the latter, while disregarding or modifying the former." (Douglas Johnston and Cynthia Sampson, *Religion: The Missing Dimension of Statecraft*, Oxford University Press, New York, 1994, p. 309)

RECOMMENDATION AND CONCLUSION.

As long as poverty persists, political ambitions prevail, religious differences are stressed, violent cultures are upheld, and ethnic marginalization continues, we should expect more religious violence in the near future in Nigeria. Also the practice of demonizing each other, passed on from one generation to another, suggests that the future of coexistence in Nigeria is bleak. The situation can change if the stakeholders (Christians and Muslims) can empower the people by being prophetic and by helping the government to redirect its priorities toward building relationships, responding to felt needs, guaranteeing human rights, and protecting property. To do this, the following recommendations urgently need implementation:

1. There is a need for a reconciliation commission to investigate past wounds and to help confession, repentance, compensation, and forgiveness. This commission should learn from the weaknesses and strengths of past commissions to put in place structures that bring about true reconciliation and transformation of conflict. Also there is a need for trauma healing or healing services for all victims and offenders across the board.

2. If the Scriptures call their followers to love their enemies and to value no compulsion in religion, believers must either accept the way of nonviolence or abandon their affirmation of scriptural authority.

3. Both Christians and Muslims need to know that God is not at any point in need of their help. In fact, the truth one professes does not need to be protected. Someone said, "Any truth that needs violence to survive is not worth the truth."

4. Both Christians and Muslims should come up with forums where different theological thoughts are discussed frankly and dialogues take place to correct misconceptions and stereotypes.

5. Both Muslims and Christians should maximize the concept of tolerance. People must learn to accept other people the way they are and regard them as fellow human beings with dignity, created in God's image and likeness.

6. Both Christians and Muslims need to be creative in coming up with programs and practices that will enable interactions among people of different faiths, different ethnic groups, different regions, different clans, and different political classes and parties. This includes such practices as rural development programs, leadership training programs, poverty alleviation programs, and peacebuilding training programs with vital nonviolence tactics that will promote social interaction among peoples. The availability of technology invites us to think of creative ways Christians and Muslims in Nigeria might promote peace. We should use the media and new technology to promote peace and even to provoke people's thinking toward the development and adoption of nonviolent culture.

7. Both Christians and Muslims need to identify and name the common enemy. What is the common enemy for both religions? Is it the abuse of power by the ruling class? Is it poverty or illiteracy? Is it environmental degradation or congestion of our cities? We must educate people about the danger of war, but first we must have a vision. Our vision must rely on good and cordial relationships and embrace the humanity in the other person. It should be a call for acceptance, tolerance, coexistence, living exemplary lives, and the restoration and protection of our environment. It should also be a call for a complete reorientation of our minds, our languages, and our perceptions of other people and what they believe.

8. Both formal and informal educational activities focused on nonviolence must be injected into the Nigerian system. The primary goal is to build a new Nigeria in which political, economic, and educational powers are balanced within our civil society. The training and mobilization of both governmental and religious actors in promoting nonviolent activities for peacemaking endeavors need to be stressed.

9. The role of both Christians and Muslims is to maintain a prophetic voice in the Nigerian civil society, ensuring justice, equity, and respect for human dignity. We must say "No" to being used to kill each other. We must be concerned with seeking integrated power to shape our environment in ways that benefit all Nigerians.

28

THE DAY OF FORGIVENESS IN BURKINA FASO

Siaka Traore (Burkina Faso)

SHARING STORIES OF PEACEMAKING is happening at exactly the right time, because Africa is going through times of severe crisis. Let me tell you the story of Burkina Faso. Twenty years ago the name of our country was changed from Upper Volta to Burkina Faso, a name which means "the land of men with integrity." Completely surrounded by other countries in West Africa, Burkina Faso has a land area of 260,000 square kilometers and a population of 15 million, with another 3 million of our countrymen living in Ivory Coast.

Among the countries served by the United Nations development program, Burkina Faso is one of the three poorest, just ahead of Sierra Leone and Niger. In its recent history, Burkina Faso has undergone a number of very severe political upheavals. On August 5, 1960, it became free from France's colonial control. In 1966 it had its first coup d'etat. In 1980, it experienced its second coup d'etat. The third was in 1982. In 1983, Thomas Sankara became the president. In 1987, he was killed, and his best or second-best friend became president.

That means that in twenty years of independence there were five coup d'etats. Between 1966 and 1991, Burkina Faso was ruled by a totalitarian regime. In 1990 at a summit meeting in France, Francois Mitterand, president of France, said that without democracy there would be no bilateral assistance for any country linked to France. So

Burkina Faso headed down the pathway toward democracy like a number of other countries. From 1960 until the National Day of Forgiveness, there were a number of persecutions, many killings, torture, injustice, crime, and all sorts of attacks on the dignity of human beings. Between 1960 until March 3, 2001, which was the National Day of Forgiveness, there have been a number of events that have remained as wounds in the lives of the people of Burkina Faso. One example is the death of Thomas Sankara and later the death of two of his friends. These leaders were killed by someone they considered their best friend. All of these events from our past have contributed to what became a major crisis.

To these troubles and many others we can add the disgraceful death of the journalist Norbert Zongo and three of his friends, all killed and then burned in their car on December 13, 1998. Zongo, who was director of the newspaper *The Independent*, was investigating the death of the car driver of the president's younger brother. Everything until the death of Zongo seemed ordered by the president's family circle. Zongo's death was the last straw. The entire country went into chaos and confusion with everyone crying, "Too much is too much!" The whole country went up in flames to denounce this injustice, the injustice of the government. For seven months the country went through a crisis which seemed in all respects like a civil war. A large number of acts of vandalism and violence spread throughout the country.

As we said at the beginning, Burkina Faso is among the poorest countries in the world. If it fell into civil war, what could possibly become of it? I believe this was what God was seeing. Somehow God in his grace permitted the president to adopt a position of humility and to understand that things were going badly for the country. The president came to understand that the military intimidation through arrests and armed presence could no longer respond to the people's needs. He understood that there was crisis. So he asked a group of wise people to analyze the situation and propose solutions. This group of sixteen included three former presidents, two Catholic bishops, two pastors, two Muslim imams, two heads of traditional religions, and five well-respected elderly people. The group was chaired by the Catholic bishop, a man well-known for his stand on peace and justice. In this way the church came to play a determining role in the history of our country, especially in peacebuilding.

The council of respected persons worked for forty-five days to analyze the national situation. To find an adequate solution, the council did not simply settle for understanding the situation that confronted them. They went all the way back to the roots of the crisis, to all of the problems from 1960 to 1999. They paid attention to the various aspects of the development of the crisis. First, concerning culture and society, they noted there was a total absence of social justice, a total inequality in how natural and social resources were distributed. The result was poverty, unemployment, frustration, and bitterness.

The council also looked at political and administrative areas. They found a lack of democracy. There was political violence, in speech as well as in deed. The social structure had been politicized, and the president's party effectively controlled all of the political organizations. They also looked at economic factors and noted an absence of transparency in management of public concerns. There were a number of problems in the political climate and inequality in availability and use of public revenues.

The council also looked at ethics and noted that there had been a loss in the character of humans and in consideration of how we are human. There was a loss of moral values such as righteousness, integrity, honor, dignity, and honesty. There was a total loss of the professional sense of conscience. They also noted the number of bloody crimes: people who had been killed in coup d'etats, people who had been killed to even political scores, people who had died because of neglect or torture, and people who had disappeared because of kidnapping or arrests. They denounced economic crimes, misappropriation of public funds, and corruption in all of its forms.

In addition to all of this analysis, the group made recommendations and proposed practical solutions. Their work stopped at this point, but they set in motion another stage of the process by recommending the creation of a commission called Truth and Justice for National Reconciliation. This second stage is now in the process of resolving the crisis. The commission prepared political texts and created the proposal for a National Day of Forgiveness. Let me cite what was said by the commission concerning forgiveness: "Pardon does not signify the end of judicial action. Truth and justice cannot be brought about by command."

On the National Day of Forgiveness the leaders of the country were requested to ask forgiveness for all of the evils that the state had committed. They were requested to ask forgiveness of the victims, the parents of the victims, and the victims of political violence. Here are some excerpts from the president's message on this special day on August 4, 2001:

On this particular moment, as President of Burkina Faso, maintaining the continuity of the state, we request forgiveness and express our profound regret for the torture, the crimes, the injustice, the abuses and all the other mistakes committed by the residents of Burkina Faso on other residents of Burkina Faso. On this historic moment, we think particularly about the parents of all of the victims prematurely taken away from the love of their families.

On that noteworthy and symbolic day, the organizers of the event released hundreds of doves and white pigeons, a symbol of the return of peace to Burkina Faso. This happened at the stadium in the presence of 30,000 people, including family members of victims and various diplomats.

Because he felt it was important not only to ask verbally for pardon but also to follow words with deeds, the president addressed the nation and promised certain things. The government would make an accounting of all of the violence since 1960. Its officials would appoint committees to visit the parents and families of the victims to ask forgiveness personally, to extend understanding for the sufferings of these families, and to find out what they expected of the state. Many of these families simply wanted to know how their family member was killed. They wanted to know where the bodies of their family members were. There were a number of investigations to be able to identify bodies and graves, very sad and hard work. There were also moral reparations and material and financial restitution. There was a committee appointed to follow up on all these details to make sure the decisions were carried out. I personally became involved in the committee of people who were following up on the details.

Unfortunately, in the past our political leaders would say many things but break their promises. The follow-up committee was charged with monitoring the government, following behind saying, "You did this. You now have to do this." Hundreds of people were paid back or helped out, and others were rehabilitated. The process is ongoing. Where work has not made much progress is in the area of economic crimes. How can we punish those who made off with the state's money? Our committee is attempting to do that very thing.

This process of forgiveness has so far been able to keep Burkina Faso from entering a new cycle of violence. Someone has said that a bad arrangement is better than a good trial and I think that's where we are now. We believe that this process of forgiveness will be able to produce significant results.

29

RESPONDING TO LOOTING IN THE CONGO

Cathy Mputu (Congo)

WHAT DOES THE BIBLE SAY ABOUT LOOTING? Looting was a common practice in Old Testament times, as we see in such passages as Isaiah 8:1-4, 2 Kings 7, and 1 Samuel 15. Because of the sin of idolatry, Israel was subjected to looting by such external enemies as the Assyrians. Then in the 2 Kings text, the children of Israel looted the abandoned Assyrian camp. God allowed this to happen so as to fulfill the word of his prophets. And we are probably familiar with the text in 1 Samuel 15 that tells the story of the rejection of King Saul. He disobeyed the prophet Samuel's order to destroy the pillaged goods and all the survivors after his victory over the Amalakites.

From this perspective, we can see that looting was a form of God's judgment to punish his people or a foreign people. In Congo, destruction and theft served the same purpose. From God's perspective, looting is to be condemned, which is the reason that Reverend Diafwila-dia-Mbwangi, national evangelist of the Church of Christ in Zaire, published a tract entitled, "Zacchaeus and His Ill-Gotten Goods," based on the text from Luke 19:1-9. We need to follow the example of Zaccheus, who responded affirmatively to Jesus' invitation and showed the depth of his commitment to Jesus by making restitution for his ill-gotten wealth as a tax collector. Because of his complete obedience, Zacchaeus and his household were saved.

The same challenge faces those who would follow Jesus today. Are we prepared to restore the goods and the money to those we have robbed? After reading Mbwangi's tract, several residents of Kinshasa placed their looted goods in the Centennial Cathedral in obedience to Christ. This was one way of helping to assure that peace in the Congo would not be threatened again by uncivil behavior.

Where are the Mennonite churches on the issue of looting? What are they saying? We are grateful that the Mennonite churches have faced this challenge as peacemaking churches should. And taking that stand has opened the way for us to push forward with conflict resolution and peace. We have an even greater challenge ahead of us—to get rid of all suffering and to work toward peace in the sense of promoting the well-being of all the people of Congo.

30

ADDRESSING VIOLENCE IN ZIMBABWE

Albert Ndlovu (Zimbabwe)

WHAT ARE WE DOING AS A CHURCH to respond to violence? We are be-ginning to wake up ten years later, unfortunately. But thank God we are at last awakening. We are mobilizing the pastors from the areas that are affected by the violence. We are training them in working with the victims, and we are beginning to see results from the train-ing. In some situations people had been asked to bring their neigh-bors together to be killed. We are helping communities deal with the problem of mass graves that are scattered all over, particularly in the west side of Matebeleland. We go and find out if these people have some needs. Some people are saying we need to help them cover over the mass graves, so we are raising money for cement and other sup-plies for this purpose. Others say that we need to help them compile the history of the people that lie in these graves; this will be a large project.

How does the church work on the larger conflict and with other people who are part of the conflict? The Zimbabwe Council of Churches, the Evangelical Fellowship of Zimbabwe, and the Zim-babwe Bishop's Conference are working with other groups to deter-mine what we can do. What makes this dialogue difficult is that the government of Zimbabwe has done everything it can to hinder healthy discussion in the public space. Human rights organizations now cannot speak. Legislation has been passed to place limits on our civil liberties. And the church is the only place where people can actually speak, to use our space to address the pressing issues of our society.

So the churches are providing space for the other organizations concerned about the problems. And the various church organizations have decided to appeal to the government and to the opposition and to say to them, "We need a solution in this country. We need to speak to one another." I happen to be heading the secretariat of that particular initiative. It's ongoing, but it's not as effective as we had hoped it would be due to political factors. The church leaders have been seeking an opportunity to meet with the leaders of the opposition as well as to meet the government.

The problem we face is that the government has hindered the dialogue by insisting that the opposition should recognize them as the current government. But the opposition has refused to do that, and a stalemate has resulted. Efforts are underway to solve the problem, but we don't know how this will be done. Officials from other African governments are trying to help, and they're putting a lot of pressure on the government of Zimbabwe to sincerely address the issues. We're heading for parliamentary elections this coming March, which may provide an opportunity for the people's voice to be heard in favor of negotiations and peace.

The church is heavily involved right now in trying to solve the situation in Zimbabwe. Our hope is that together we can persuade the government to face the issues and begin moving Zimbabwe toward democracy. Please pray for us in these challenging and perilous opportunities to be peacemakers.

31

ENGAGING TRAUMATIC BARRIERS

Cecile Nyiramana (Rwanda)

I HAVE BEEN ASKED TO TELL THE STORY of my personal experiences in the times of violent conflict in Rwanda. Since our themes include healing, forgiveness, and renewal, I will try in a few words to tell what I went through during the genocide and what I did after my healing.

I was a student at the university when the genocide came upon us. I was studying with my husband, and we went through rough times, but we were able to survive them. We were traumatized, as was everyone. And after the genocide, we hadn't yet gotten past our trauma.

The greatest trauma of all was my husband's arrest and imprisonment. To this day he is in prison. At first, I couldn't accept the situation. I was traumatized by the events I was experiencing and seeing. We had been tested together in a number of ways, but his imprisonment traumatized me far more than anything we had yet undergone. We have two young children and I didn't know how I would be able to raise the children alone, especially because of my trauma.

The answer to my problems came in the form of help from the people of the Friends church. I wasn't even a member of the Friends church, but the people came to me to see if they could help. They helped me to understand that Christ is the Prince of Peace. They invited me to their seminars on conflict management. They helped me find work and that helped me move past my trauma. And that was when I began to wonder, "Is God watching over me?" After I was healed, I realized that God had a plan for me. So I told myself that I needed to do something for others traumatized as I was.

My experiences remind us that it is necessary to move beyond our trauma. There are so many others who were and still are traumatized. These are the people we need to find because they know peace is necessary—but don't know how to find it on their own. These are the people who will fight for peace because they've suffered so much from violence. You can speak of peace, but if you haven't known violence, what can you do for it? If you want to fight for peace and you encounter threats to peace, you can easily just let things go on like they are. And that is why today I am fighting for peace in Rwanda: because I know the horrors of violence.

After much prayer and asking God what I could do in Rwanda, I came to the understanding that because God had given me grace and peace, I could share it with others. Then I got the idea to address the needs of a particular combination of people. There are two categories of women: those who have husbands assumed to be guilty and are therefore in prison, and widows who escaped the genocide themselves but lost their husbands. As you can understand, these women didn't want to speak to each other. Yet I knew we needed to break down the walls, to try to get them together, and to open a dialogue between them.

You must remember that it is especially women who undergo the consequences of war. They are the ones raped during war. They are the heads of households when their husbands have died, as in Rwanda. I believe that when the women are changed, all of society is changed. If women come together, sit together, and speak about the possibilities of peace, I'm convinced that the men will follow. But the problem is that the widows and the wives of those in prison have nothing with which they can support their families. You have to find material aid, even as you are moving them beyond trauma and teaching them about conflict management. If they continue to have economic problems, it's very hard to speak with them meaningfully about peace.

Through our Friends Peace House we're looking everywhere to find ways to help these women. We began work with a group of thirty women and now have two more groups, so we are working with a total of ninety women. Our goal is to eventually have cell groups of women throughout Rwanda. This is an ambitious goal, but when we have been saved by the grace of our Lord, we must do everything we can for peace. Please pray for us in bringing about a new and peaceful Rwanda.

32

TRANSFORMING CONFLICT

Adamu Buba (Nigeria)

CONFLICT IS CONSIDERED IN MOST PARTS OF THE WORLD, including Nigeria, to be abnormal. Yet conflict is a part of life. Every plural society is bound to experience one or another form of conflict. One definition of conflict is that it is "a struggle over values and claims to scarce status, power and resources in which the aims of the opponents are to neutralize or eliminate their rivals." In this sense, conflict may be conceptualized as a way of settling problems originating from opposing interests.

However, conflict need not be portrayed as warfare or violence. What is to be emphasized, therefore, is not conflict per se but the way one responds to it. Conflict need not follow a negative course. If constructively handled, it can become an agent of growth and development for all parties. To this extent, conflict is not to be demonized but rather is to be confronted with efficient procedures for cooperative problem solving. It is when it is not properly and sincerely confronted that conflict can lead to violence. Conflict must be resolved, transformed, or managed to ensure social justice and peace between individuals and groups having divergent interests.

Some causes of conflicts in Nigeria are disagreements about farm land, the establishment of local governments, the location of the local government headquarters, the location of markets, the building of churches and mosques, cultural influences, and the authority of chiefs. Since the introduction of Islam in Nigeria, the Hausa Fulani have considered themselves its guardians. They regard non-Muslims as unbelievers and infidels. With the advent of Christianity in the twentieth century, its followers built many churches. Rather than breeding conflict, the processes of Christianity further cemented the relationship between communities, individuals, and their leaders.

Causes and spheres of conflict in Nigeria can also be summarized like this:

- competition for land, space, and resources;
- the disputed jurisdiction of certain traditional rulers and chiefs;
- the creation of local government and the location of their headquarters;
- ethnic and individual or sectional competition over access to scarce political and economic resources;
- micro and macro social structures;
- population growth and expansionist tendencies;
- the pollution of cultural practices.

In most of the conflict areas in the northern part of Nigeria, God intervened through the religious leaders to control the conflicts which had degenerated into violence. The typical example of this occurred during the Zangon Kataf and Mangu Bokkos communal crisis. While many lives were lost, God used the Christian leaders to show that if conflict is managed, its escalation can be avoided. We can maintain the respect for life and property that God commands us to uphold.

Whenever a conflict has resulted in violence, appeals have been made to the combatants by traditional rulers, religious leaders, and pressure groups to stop the killings. Preventive measures must be taken in other cities to avoid the escalation and spread of the conflict to other parts of the country.

Several local and national conflict resolution efforts have been initiated. These include the effort of the Christian Association of Nigeria (CAN). The disputants must come to understand that a conflict can be a learning process because it creates an opportunity for people to know each other better and to live together by tolerating and accommodating each other's strength and weakness. People need to come together to find common ground.

In conclusion, the reality of social interaction and community relationships in Africa in the field of conflict resolution, transformation, and management needs to be handled with utmost care. The structure and process of government and its mode and degree of efficiency of resources management are critical factors in reducing conflict based on ethnic, class, gender, religion, and other factors. We should bear in mind that conflict resolution is intended to change or help the course of a conflict. Churches have to recognize their primary responsibility to resolve conflict that can lead to violence within the context of their spiritual covenant for the maintenance of peace in the country and even the continent at large.

33

SEEK THE
PEACE OF THE CITY

Scott Holland (USA)

IN A WORLD OF HARSH IDEOLOGIES, tribalism, and clashes between fighting gods, it is well to remember that Jesus, whom the biblical witness calls the Prince of Peace, often comes to us as a stranger. Of course Jesus also comes to us as a friend. It is wonderful to know Jesus as a friend, and indeed, we do know Jesus as a friend. But likewise it is marvelous to be surprised when Jesus comes to us as a stranger.

There is a great temptation in any religion to domesticate the divine and thus make God our own family, churchly, tribal, or national deity. The genius of the Judeo-Christian tradition's representation of God is seen in the diverse stories through which the divine presence in history is presented as both familiar and totally other or strange. I would suggest that as we work for peace in a broken world we need to be attentive to the times when Jesus comes to us as a stranger.

The Hebrew Bible presents us with the astonishing story of Melchizedek. He was not of the tribe, clan, or faith of father Abraham. He came out of the desert as a stranger to the tent of Abraham, offering a gift of bread and wine. Abraham warmly greeted the priest from this far country and communed with him as bread was broken and wine poured. Abraham even paid Melchizedek a tithe before sending him on his way. This man, Melchizedek, was a stranger priest from the far country.

The New Testament writer of the Book of Hebrews offers a shocking interpretation of this Melchizedek narrative. We are told that Jesus is not really like the proper priest from the lines of Aaron and Levi; instead he is more like Melchizedek. He is more like a stranger priest from the far country in this story. This story helps us remember that we must be attentive and respectful toward the stranger, the other, the alien, even the heretic. It helps us remember that a religion that fails to love the stranger becomes a source of terror rather than transformation in the world.

A peace church in the world not only cares for its own members—its friends—but is committed to creating public spaces and democratic politics hospitable to strangers from the far country. These strangers may represent different tribes, religions, philosophies, and lifestyles. The Historic Peace Churches have led the way in presenting the doctrine of separation of church and state as foundational for a public peace. The peace churches have resisted theocratic temptations, whether embodied in the theologies and politics of Constantinianism, radical Zionism, or Sharia Law. We are committed to a public peace. We are committed to seeking the shalom of the city. We are concerned with the ministry of reconciliation in all of life, whether we find ourselves in the sanctuary or in the city streets.

I would like for us to meditate on the vision of the prophet Jeremiah. The prophet's vision and voice calls us to be peacemakers in the world for the world. The prophet Jeremiah calls us to a kind of worldly holiness as he tells the people of God living in exile to seek the peace of the city. The Jews, the people of God, were living in exile in Babylon, and some felt they could not sing the Lord's song in a strange land—that it was necessary to return to Jerusalem to the holy city, to the high and exalted mountain. The prophet Jeremiah said, "Some day you will return, but for now this is what you shall do. You shall build houses and live in them. You shall take husbands and wives and have sons and daughters and seek the shalom, the peace of the city, for in its peace you shall find your peace."

It is crucial to remember that this city to which the prophet refers is not Jerusalem but in the land of Babylon. We are called to seek cultures of peace in this world. Thus, we do more than preach peace and protest war. We build houses and we live in them. We plant gardens and joyfully eat the produce. With hope we take partners and lovingly have sons and daughters. We are called to seek the welfare of the city. For in seeking the welfare of the city or the common good, we find our good lives. So this call, this prophetic call, is a call to cultural engagement, to an experience of a being a living peace church in a blessed yet broken world. Thus our salvation, our redemption, must touch all of life, and it must touch life in ways that lead to reconciliation—not only between the solitary individual and God, but also between solitary souls and society.

The relationship of soul to society or the movement from the sanctuary to the streets is admittedly complicated and challenging. We are now seeing a rise of global fundamentalism. Many fundamentalists, whether Muslim or Christian, feel they have a God's-eye-view of the world and therefore a right and responsibility to impose their will on other people. They seek to impose their religion and politics on the entire public square.

We in the peace church traditions have an important phrase, "No force in religion." Therefore, even if we feel we have seen the truth, we do not impose that truth with the force of either the sword or the autocratic statute. This is the reason the separation of church and state is so important. In a democratic state there must be hospitable space for a diversity of persons, politics, and religions. In seeking cultures of peace we realize the importance of public spaces where a great diversity of expression is welcome.

We embrace the peaceful tradition of no force in religion, but we do not retreat to sacred reservations. We know that to truly love the neighbor means that one is called to take some responsibility for the neighbor's history and well-being. The idea of a public theology is really rooted in this metaphor of seeking the shalom and the welfare of the city. We are not to simply seek the welfare of our tribe, clan, denomination, or church, because as ambassadors for Christ, we are given the ministry of reconciliation in the entirety of the broken world. But it is a challenge. It is an enormous challenge.

There is great promise in thinking about public space and our contribution to public life, assuming it will be pluralistic. I am suggesting that we support government systems that are deeply democratic and provide public space in which respect and dignity are extended even to those who are the other, the stranger. A pressing question for us in the peace churches is how we go public with our faith. How do we enter the public square?

I am not simply talking about evangelism; I am talking about a productive involvement in the public good. There are times when the Holy Spirit can lead us in a public discourse that isn't heavy with God talk but is nevertheless spiritually wise and informed by the gospel of life and reconciliation. Our language matters so much that our discourse, our stories, our words, must take on flesh again and again as we seek the peace of the city.

There have been occasions when the public space has not been hospitable to the church. One clear instance is the issue of conscientious objection, the refusal to bear arms in the military. There were great tensions in the United States, especially during World War I. However, that tension led to a great deal of public activism, reminding the government that in a bona fide democracy, space must be provided for the convictions of those who cannot kill. Thus, eventually the system of alternative service was created through which persons could pursue a peaceful means to a public good.

How does one have a public peace without a spiritual peace? I would answer this question in two ways. It is crucial to have spiritual peace, a peace with God, before we can go public with the witness of peace. This is a central Christian affirmation, and few would quarrel with this teaching.

Yet I think this answer is too easy. Too many people spend a great deal of time cultivating their own private peace without finding that this leads them to care for the public good. Personal peace and public peace must certainly go together, but personal peace doesn't always begin in solitude. It might, but at times it might also begin in public service to others. Return again to the challenge, to the vision of the prophet Jeremiah. He tells us that when we are seeking the peace of the city, the welfare of the city of Babylon, when we are pursuing that public good, then we find our own peace.

So we do need both spiritual and public peace. Sometimes shalom begins with a personal, spiritual experience of peace that goes public. Other times, it is attending to the public good that brings to us the strange gift, the unexpected gift, of spiritual peace. We seek the shalom of the city because as a peace church we are indeed called to be in the world for the welfare of the world.

PRAYER
OLIVER KISAKA SIMIYU (KENYA)

Lord, while you are seeking to use us to reach others, we have our own struggles. In your love use us despite our weakness. We also know today that you are walking with us, helping us to grow and to walk in that same gospel, that we may not promote to others what we do not have. May we share with others what gives them an opportunity to know the King of Kings, the Prince of Peace.

Father, we pray for all people on the earth, especially those who do not seem to appreciate the gospel, that they may know it is meant for them. I know that there is so much that you have in store for us. Enrich each one of us. Empower each one of us. Enlighten each one of us. Renew us to serve you. Thank you, Lord. In Jesus' name we pray. Amen. God bless us all.

PART VI
THE COURAGE TO HOPE

Stories and meditations about hope amid violence

34

WALKING IN
THE GOSPEL OF PEACE

Oliver Kisaka Simiyu (Kenya)

WHAT SHOULD CHRISTIANS SENSE when they listen to God, when they read from the Scriptures? What perspective should a Christian take in the face of the many challenges facing our continent? The situation Africa finds herself in, or that we as Africans have brought on ourselves, speaks so loudly it makes one wonder whether there is any hope for Africa at all. But as I read the Scriptures, the message I get there is not one of despair but of hope.

My comments are based on Acts 10, dealing with Peter's role in bringing peace to Cornelius. The peace that God brings to us through Jesus is a peace that has been in his plan since before creation. Paul says as much in the first chapter of Ephesians. Paul, who was very fond of discussing the pre-creation planning of God, talks about the salvation God gave before the foundation of the world. In 2 Timothy 1:9, he talks about a God of purpose and of planning.

When Christ comes, Christ is not an afterthought of God. Christ is not an accident. He is not Plan B. He is not a strategy of a God who has been caught unawares by a situation that has gone sour. Christ comes in God's time. He comes when God said he would come.

What happens before that? A lot happens. Human beings have the opportunity to experiment with their free will. When God says free will, he really means free. He will warn you and say this is wrong or that is wrong, but you are responsible. You are in charge. So Adam cannot say it was the woman's idea. You have free will. You are responsible. You take up a gun to shoot somebody. You are the killer. Don't say the devil made you do it.

Before Christ, we see God's demonstration of what can happen if God decides to judge human wrongdoing. The case of Noah shows that we are alive by God's mercy, by God's withholding of his wrath. It's not that God cannot create better human beings. Rather, God chooses to love us and loves us so thoroughly that he walks with us through our failures, through our struggles, waiting for Christ.

At the right time, Christ comes. Who is Christ? God himself. God has revealed himself to us. And when he reveals himself, he is the Prince of Peace. All governance shall be upon his shoulders. He is the God who, when he reigns in his kingdom, brings to all the subjects the ability to enjoy life to the fullest.

So the story of Cornelius is to me an amazing one—and fits so well the theme of the conference on which this book is based. In verses 34-36 we read, "Then Peter began to speak to them: 'I truly understand that God shows no partiality, but in every nation anyone who fears him and does what is right is acceptable to him. You know the message he sent to the children of Israel, preaching peace by Jesus Christ—he is Lord of all'" (KJV). This is Peter's conclusion. But how many conclusions did Peter need to come to?

My subject is "Walking in the gospel of Peace." God in his amazing love and wisdom always speaks to ordinary people amid challenging circumstances. I have found that it is easier for people to talk about their problems than their successes. If I complained to you about being really sick, most likely you would tell me, "I've been suffering as well." If I were to tell you how broke I am, likely you would tell me, "You know, I've got this loan to pay, and I've got this and I've got that." I don't know of any human being who doesn't face trials, challenges, difficulties, and setbacks, day after day.

Yet God calls people in those circumstances; God sends people on "missions impossible." He helps people accomplish things which in their own strength they might never have thought of or done. And many times God's interest is in the person he's using. Yes, it's important for those people, but what about the messenger? Will I be a messenger who publishes peace I don't have? Will I export what is no good for home consumption? Many times Peter struggled with grace. Had you interviewed Peter for the job of director of Jesus' disciples, I'm sure you would not have hired him. He failed too many times.

But isn't that the wisdom of God, the unlimited nature of the God that we serve? When you are deciding you are nothing is when God decides he is going to use nothing and make nothing an instrument of God's effectiveness. In the process, God changes this nothing into something. Peter was there when Jesus told the sea, "Peace, be still." And the Bible indicates that he said, "Whoa! So I was beside the Son of God."

Then take the case of Cornelius. God wanted to bring the gospel of peace to Cornelius. He wanted to use somebody who knew the gospel, but to get Peter from his home to Cornelius' house was a major task. When Peter was hungry, God sent him a sheet filled with all sorts of four-footed animals and told him, "Peter, kill and eat."

But Peter was thoroughly schooled in the law of Moses. He had mastered the rules, the systems of thinking, and the rigid principles. "I know how God works. I will not kill a thing." Three times Peter refused the solution to his hunger. Later he came to discover God's message. What God has cleansed, don't call common. If God has cleansed something, don't make a fool of yourself by opposing it.

Reluctantly Peter went to Cornelius' house. He was quite honest with Cornelius, confessing, "I really did not want to come, but the Lord sent me." Peter's life is interesting. How many times Peter had to be broken and broken again to be helped to see that what matters most is what God has decided to do. And God has decided that whoever comes to know Jesus will walk in peace.

Today we struggle with much interesting terminology. I call it interesting—not because I uphold what is advocated, but because as I listen it seems that a primary purpose is keeping the gospel at bay. We would like human rights without the gospel. We would like equitable distribution without the gospel. We would like development without the gospel. Don't infringe on other people's rights. So many "don'ts." As if to make sure that those who have the gospel of peace should not share it. Yet when Peter went to the house of Cornelius, he found that Cornelius was not a rowdy man; he was one of the good people.

God is concerned about peace that is holistic. If you find two people on the street fighting, as a peacemaker you separate them. But if you don't talk to them, you will need to separate them tomorrow. That's what the gospel of Jesus is saying. If you want to help these people, go farther than just telling them to stop fighting. Tell them, "You people, why were you created? Do you know the Lord Jesus? Do you have peace in your heart? Do you know that what you're fighting for can be found right inside your heart?"

Contentment is a matter of choice. You can choose to live simply and be satisfied. It's a matter of choice. For Peter that day, what he was being asked to shared was so precious. He had thought it was for Jews only. Now Peter shared with Cornelius, who seemed to gain something so much more important than anything he'd ever experienced.

Let me highlight four aspects of the story of Peter and Cornelius. First, Peter knew Jesus personally and had peace in his heart. Peace is not possible unless we open our lives to know God in truth, and in his wisdom God has chosen that that truth is found in Christ.

A concern here, however, is whether it is possible to proclaim Christ as the truth and not be seen as intolerant. I want to ask a serious question: Is it possible that Christ has said, "I am the way, the truth and the life. No one can come to the Father except [through] me?" Is it possible to believe that? The whole world is struggling with these questions. As I see it, we have lost the God of tensions, the God who holds judgment in one hand and love in the other and does not make them inconsistent. This is the God who is both eternal and particular. He is transcendent, but he also dwells in our hearts.

Humans find it difficult to relate to this kind of God. So when I talk to my Muslim brothers, they see me as intolerant because I have told them there is life in Christ. I must sort that out in my heart. If they do not have that peace, they cannot understand it unless I help them understand. This connects with the fact that the tolerant/intolerant card is being played all over the world. One might think that Christians are the most intolerant people on earth. We must wrestle with that, because sometimes we will need to cause conflict so people come to know Christ. We will need to tell them, "I appreciate what you believe, but have you ever heard. . .?"

Second, Peter was committed to following Christ despite the struggles. I am impressed that Peter followed Jesus. He struggled, he failed, but he kept following. I think his most difficult experience was in the Garden of Gethsemane. He really wanted to defend Jesus. He took his sword and chopped off the ear of one of the men. But in that act also came his greatest shock, because the person he was trying to defend took the ear from the ground and put it back, and Peter began to realize how wrong he had been. Yet after that we see him denying Jesus. He made mistakes, but he kept following.

Third, Peter was available to share the gospel of peace. The sharing is indiscriminate: to the hungry, food; to the naked, clothes; to the fighting, separation and reconciliation. But we must also let those with whom we share know that when you have peace in your heart, external fighting begins to lose its appeal. Let's not be ashamed to share that gospel.

My fourth and last point is that Peter was willing to forsake all for the gospel. It is not possible to live a full life on this earth if we are in love with mammon, if we are in love with material things, if we are in love with what this world has to offer. It's just not possible. The attitude of true Christians must be totally different. We will have jobs. We will buy land. We will send our children to school. But what if those things were not there? What if they were taken away? What if the Lord said, "Leave Jerusalem and go to Cornelius' house?" What if the Lord said that today he wants us to go bear testimony in Iraq? Such questions about our readiness to forsake all for the gospel are at the root of what it means to be a peacemaker.

If two people are fighting and I come between them, it's obvious what will happen. Some of the blows will strike me. Am I ready? I think Peter was ready. It was costly to him, but he still went to Cornelius' house. After that he had to answer serious questions from the disciples. Others had not been through the experiences he had. He had to keep pleading with them, "Please, what could I have done? The Holy Spirit himself did it."

May the Lord grant us grace as we walk in the gospel of peace. May we choose to be peacemakers. The choice, essentially, is to become dead people. The apostle Paul said he gladly gave up his life so another might have peace. May the Lord grant us grace and bless our hearts with his presence. May the gospel of peace free us from the guilt that can result from failure. May the gospel help us to realize that if God could use Peter, God can use each of us.

35

THE MEANING OF PEACE

Matthew Abdullahi Gali (Nigeria)

PEACE, ACCORDING TO THE *New Concise Bible Dictionary*, is in the Hebrew *shalom*, which means completeness, soundness, and well-being. It also means material possessions. As Psalm 122:6-9 states, "Pray for the peace of Jerusalem. May those who love you be secure. May there be peace within your walls and security with your citadels. For the sake of our brothers and friends, I will say peace be within you. For the sake of the house of the Lord our God, I will seek your prosperity" (NIV). The Bible says also that a man reaps what he sows. When we sow peace, we reap peace with tranquility. But when we sow discord, either directly or unintentionally, we reap discord and turbulence, the opposite of tranquility. When there is turbulence, everybody suffers.

Peace brings good health even during old age, according to Genesis 15:15, whereas crisis leads to poor health. Poor health does not respect any religious deed or profession. That is why the Bible says to seek and pursue peace, according to Psalm 34:14.

Quietness is related to good health. Where there is peace we live quiet lives, free from the pandemonium and fear around us. This quietness pleases God, according to 1 Timothy 2:2-3. If it pleases God, then it is imperative for Christians and Muslims to practice it among us.

Where there is peace there is sanity. The Bible tells the story of an insane man who robbed his community of its peace as he terrorized its residents. When Jesus healed him, his sanity was restored and peace prevailed (Mark 5:1-15). When a mob is stirred up into rampage and rage, they behave insanely. If there is no security, lives and properties are lost, leaving behind orphans and widows. There are unwanted deaths on both sides. Often deep indelible scars are left.

When Jesus taught his followers and listeners he said, "Blessed are the peacemakers, for they will be called children of God." In other words, we prove that we belong to God, according to Matthew 5:9, when we live in peace, and God blesses us for that. God even says that we should not avenge evil for evil but rather return good for evil (Rom. 12:17-18) and show love even to our enemies (Matt. 5:44, 45). If we obey this command, then mistrust and recriminations will end, and we can live together in harmony, even while professing our different faiths.

Now we come to development. When there is peace, there is development and security for the city that trusts in the Lord, according to Isaiah 26:1-4. When there is development, both Christians and Muslims enjoy it. The opposite is degradation, deprivation, and desolation. We don't want what is happening in some parts of this world to happen to Africa.

Finally, we come to trust. The Bible admonishes us to follow peace with all men, because peace makes for trust and holiness. Suspicion is ungodly and will mar any relationship. If we don't trust ourselves, then we cannot relate to God. Suspicion hinders love, but trust engenders it. Both Christians and Muslims need love. This is crucial for our coexistence and true neighborliness.

What is the source of this peace? Having agreed that peace is an essential and necessary condition for our coexistence, we need to have an inexhaustible peace. The Bible unequivocally declares that Jesus Christ is the Prince of Peace, as is foreshadowed in Isaiah 9:6. He paid the price with his own life to make that title appropriate. It was not just conferred on him by some well-wishers.

At Christ's birth, according to Luke 2:14, the angels of heaven publicly declared peace to the whole world, which was tormented by the vicious Roman Empire. Jesus Christ offered himself to his disciplies as this peace in place of the fragile and tattered peace the world has always attempted to achieve (John 14:27). Jesus is the perfect peace for all our troubles.

36

MEDITATION AND PRAYER

Million Belete (Ethiopia)

JESUS CHRIST SAID, "BLESSED ARE THE PEACEMAKERS, for they will be called children of God." John, the disciple whom Jesus loved, says in 1 John 3:1, "How great is the love the Father has lavished on us that we should be called children of God!" (NIV). And that we are. Peacemaking is synonymous with reconciliation. There is a phrase peacemakers use over and over again, "the ministry of reconciliation." Where does this ministry of reconciliation concept come from?

Let the Word speak to your heart from 2 Corinthians 5:16-21:

> So from now on we regard no one from a human point of view, though we once regarded Christ in this way, we do so no longer. Therefore, if anyone is in Christ, he is a new creation. The old has gone. The new has come. All this is from God, who reconciled us to himself through Christ and gave us the ministry of reconciliation. That God was reconciling the world to himself in Christ, not counting men's sins against them. And he has committed to us the message of reconciliation. We are therefore Christ's ambassadors, as though God were making his appeal through us. We implore you on Christ's behalf, be reconciled to God. God made him who had no sin to be sin for us, so that in him we might become the righteousness of God. (NIV)

The first thing I want to note is that we are newly created. In fact, we are re-created by Christ because he has reconciled us to God. In the words of Jesus to Nicodemus, we are newly born. So, first and foremost, I remind myself that I am a Christian—not by name but because I am reborn. I am newly created. And I am honored to be part of the church known as a peacemaking church. I am representing a part of the body of Christ made up of believers known as peacemakers. My church is me. I am a peacemaker, and I'm a man of peace.

Are we in fact men and women of peace? Jesus is the Prince of Peace. Jesus is our King. Jesus is the head of the state we come from. This is what makes us ministers of reconciliation. 2 Corinthians 5 refers to us as ambassadors. An ambassador goes from one country to another country. We are from what country? From the country whose people are the children of God. Our citizenship is in that kingdom.

Imagine! We are the ambassadors of that king and that nation whose people are scattered all over the world. We are children of God. Let us praise our God because of who we are. Let us meditate on this and also inwardly, each of us, pray about our assignment as messengers, as reconcilers.

Let us pray this prayer: Our Father and our God, first and foremost we thank you for being our Father. You are our God. We have no other God. You are our Father and we call you "Abba," "Father." Thank you for the privilege you have given us to be called your children. Thank you for the privilege you have given to us to come to you, the creator of this earth, the creator of all of us. And, Lord, we now especially thank you that we are people of peace. Lord, thank you for the peace between us and you, for reconciling us to you. Thank you for the forgiveness of sin. Lord Jesus, you died for us. Because you died for us, we are children of God. Thank you for this fact.

Lord, thank you for appointing us as your ambassadors, your ambassadors on this planet earth, where there are so many of your children. We are mindful of our names. We have given ourselves all sorts of names, Father, but you don't look at us as Orthodox, or Baptists, or Presbyterians, or Mennonites, or Quakers. You refer to us as "my children." And we affirm that we are your children. We thank you for this fact. As your children, Lord, we are trying to learn from one another how to be better ambassadors for you on this earth, where there are many of your children.

Lord, help us. Help us to communicate with one another. Be with those who stand before us to deliver messages and to tell us what you want us to learn. Be with us as we listen. Lord, we commit our life to you, our will to you, this day that you have given to us. This day is the first day of the rest of our lives, a day to be better ambassadors for you. Lord, thank you for the promise that you will be with us. For you have said, "Where two or three are gathered in my name, I will be there." Thank you. Today we commit all our being to you and ask you to lead us in Jesus' name. Amen.

37

HIDDEN CORNERS: A MEDITATION

Steven Mang'ana (Tanzania)

Pastor Mang'ana's meditation was inspired by an article written by Pastor Jack Hayford entitled "In Front of Jesus," copyright © Jack W. Hayford, Jack Hayford Ministries 2006.

ALONG WITH OUR BODIES we also need to offer our hearts to God. We should ask and invite the Lord to search our hearts. The Psalmist says it with these words, "Search me, O God, and my heart; test me and know my anxious thoughts. See if there is any offensive way in me, and lead me in the way everlasting" (Ps. 139:23-24).

This is not the prayer of a man who at the time was in deep sin or great failure. Of course, David experienced such times. Psalm 51 is his prayer of repentance for adultery and murder. But this was not the case when David wrote Psalm 139. In the earlier verses of this psalm David speaks of God's loving hand upon his life.

He knows that the Lord is with him everywhere and all the time. He knows that God made him in a wonderful way and has a wonderful plan for his life. He goes on to say that the Lord's promises of blessing to him are like the sands of the sea in number. He is aware of God's great love, which is very precious to him in every way.

This psalm is a picture of a man who is living in fellowship with God. Yet he is asking God to search his heart and try his thoughts for some inner evil that he might not know about. This psalm tells us in the opening verses that God knows us better than we know ourselves. How wise it is to invite his search, to let him point out any dangerous areas in our lives that might bring hurt or harm to ourselves or others.

When I was a boy, my dad would give me a list of things that I was to do every Saturday. It was hard work and usually took four hours or more to finish. Then I could spend the rest of the day playing.

When Dad would come home in the evening, he would take the list and look around to see if everything had been done right. Sometimes he would point out some hidden corner not swept perfectly clean. I would take a little hand-brush and finish the job properly right then and there.

My dad was not putting me down in some unkind way. He was just helping me to learn how to do a job right the first time. When I would get the job done, he was always ready to say, "That's good work, son." As you might imagine, the next week I would remember all the hidden corners, the places I had not seen before.

It is possible for all of us to have hidden corners in our hearts that need to be swept clean. I don't say this unkindly, but many people are caught up in sinful habits of which they are not aware. They will eventually reap what they sow. In time, their sin will bring the harvest of pain and punishment. Then they will wonder, "Why did this happen to me?"

Church leaders spend many hours trying to help people with personal problems resulting from hidden sins. They are thinking, saying, and doing wrong things but don't even know it. Few people say, "I just decided I was going to turn my back on God and live a sinful life." Most of the time we come hurt and wounded on the inside because we don't know how to walk with Jesus or how to hear his voice.

If we ask the Lord to show us our hidden sins, he will speak to us and help us to sweep every little corner of our lives bright and clean. As we listen for this voice and seek to obey his word, we will learn to walk close to his word. We will learn to walk close by his side every day. Then as the night draws near, we too can hear him say, "That was a good job, son. I am really with you." And this is worth it all.

38

THEREFORE WE ARE AMBASSADORS FOR CHRIST: A SERMON

Mkoko Boseka (Congo)

BEFORE BECOMING AN AMBASSADOR FOR CHRIST, as portrayed in 2 Corinthians 5:16-21, the apostle Paul first emphasizes that humanity has been corrupted and sullied by sin. Paul underscores something crucial to show the extent to which man is corrupt. Humanity must first pass through Christ's refinery, where Jesus Christ alone is the refiner and purifier. The Lord can change lead to gold, base material into precious, sinners into saints. When we leave this refinery, which I call also the institute of diplomats, where Christ is the sole teacher, we must ask ourselves, "What credential do we have when we complete our studies? What rank are we given?" The Bible tells me that we have been granted a different status. All things have become new. We have a new vision of the world, we wear new glasses to see the world, we have new headphones to understand the world, and we have a completely different manner for reacting to the issues in the world.

As he was talking about passing through the refinery, the institute of diplomats, the apostle Paul used the conjunction "therefore." He says "Threfore we are ambassadors for Christ." We are the ambassadors of the kingdom of God in this world, the kingdom of justice in the world. Therefore we must know that education for justice is a priority for believers. It is useless to call ourselves disciples of Christ, sons of God, animated by his Spirit, if we don't make the effort to form our conscience in the spirit of justice and to collaborate effectively in all initiatives to restore justice wherever it has been violated.

My brothers and sisters in Christ, in our role as ambassadors of peace in this world, we have a crucial mission—a mission to restore respect for the image of God and to help others to accept differences of color, of race, of political party, of morphology among us, because they constitute the richness of the human spirit. These differences constitute the treasures of the image of God in us. An animal can't organize a political party. Why? Because it doesn't have this power, it's not created in God's image. But we humans, created in God's image, do have this power, the power to engage in political activity. This is the richness of the image of God.

The ambassador is named by the country's president to represent his country in another country, and he always retains his country's identity, that of his country of origin. As ambassadors of God's kingdom in this world, we must identify ourselves according to God's kingdom which we represent. Allow me to give you an example. The United States ambassador to Congo must identify himself with his country, and if he changes his nationality, if he changes his identity and becomes Congolese for his own interests, at that moment he is no longer the U.S. ambassador to Congo.

We are prophets, brothers and sisters. Our function is not to announce the future, as some are in the habit of telling us, but to speak in place of God, to speak in the name of God. In other words, in our role as God's prophets, we are God's voice. For that reason, we must not mince our words. In the Bible, what distinguishes the prophetic works from others is an expression, the "signature" often repeated, "The word of the Lord" or "Thus speaks the Lord."

We are ambassadors, prophets. We must accept the risks of our own mission. William Penn, in his book entitled *No Cross, No Crown*, says: "The cross of Christ is the pathway to Christ to gain access to the crown of Christ." Thus we are ambassadors, we are prophets. Brothers and sisters, let us strengthen ourselves for effective action, and may God bless us.

39

LIKE A DRUNKEN RAT: A MEDITATION

Bruce B. Khumalo (Zimbabwe)

LET ME BEGIN WITH A STORY. There once was a rat that lived in a house inhabited by a large cat. The ferocious cat was constantly on the prowl for the rat and was always waiting for an opportunity to pounce on him. The rat led a meager, anxious existence because there was little food in the house other than what the owner of the house gave the cat. Every morning a pan of victuals was set out for the cat, and if the rat was fortunate, he could sneak a few morsels before the cat arrived or after the cat left. However, the rat's life was in danger should the cat arrive while he was still hurriedly grubbing at the pan.

One day the home owner accidentally knocked a bottle of beer off a shelf. The spilled beer filled the cat's food pan. The rat darted for the pan, jumped in, and began to gorge himself on beer before the cat had time to appear. When the cat finally arrived, the rat was completely drunk. The cat was dismayed that the rat did not scamper away as he approached, ready to give chase. When he reached the rat, the cat was completely surprised to encounter two red bloodshot eyes looking back at him with no fear at all. In fact the reeling rat seemed ready to pounce on the cat at any moment. This so shocked the cat that he quickly left to find a safe hiding place.

The churches need to be like the drunken rat, so filled with their message of peacemaking that those around them are shocked by their fearlessness. There are many ways to describe or define peace. One can speak of the absence of physical harm and threat. One can speak of the presence of the United Nations or international troops. One can speak of reconciliation, transparency, truth, and justice. Peace goes beyond everyone keeping quiet to finding a way for those in the group to express their ideas and feelings. Therefore peace has many dimensions: vertical, horizontal, internal, and external.

Peace created by human ingenuity is less than adequate. Consider the difficulties of the Congo, Sierra Leone, Israel, Palestine, Lebanon, Syria, Iraq, the United States, and Zimbabwe. Each has attempted to create peace in different ways, but open conflict continues. Practicing peace in our daily lives can help. All of us can practice living peacefully with one another at home. We can avoid buying toy guns for children in the formative stages. We can avoid watching violent movies or using violent language. Moses wanted to start with public peace before experiencing private peace. He learned the hard way. He committed a murder and had to flee until the Lord gave him inner peace.

If we want genuine peace, we must follow the model of Jesus Christ. To choose the way of peace is to choose the way of death. We should realize that we start dying when we are born. Steven chose the way of peace and died a martyr. He said, "Behold, I see the heavens opened, and the Son of man standing at the right hand of God" (Acts 7:56). As he died, he said, "Lord, do not hold this sin against them" (Acts 7:60). This repeats the prayer of Jesus, "Father, forgive them; for they do not know what they are doing" (Luke 23:34). So Steven died peacefully, praying for the forgiveness of those who stoned him.

But let us not wait only to talk of peace after death, with words on our tombstone, "May his/her soul rest in peace." During our lifetimes may our lives be marked by a unique peace that passes human understanding. Just as the recipe for living is to keep breathing, so the recipe for peace is to develop a peaceable lifestyle. Those who say that the ends justify the means are often ready to be violent. I believe that the means shall justify the ends, so that living peacefully is necessary to achieving peace. Seek peace and pursue it. "Blessed are the peacemakers, for they will be called children of God" (Matt. 5:9).

40

A MEDITATION ON THE LORD'S PRAYER

Donald Miller (USA)

WHAT A REMARKABLE EXPERIENCE IT IS to be with people from different traditions, places, and languages praying the Lord's Prayer together! Because the prayer is being voiced in the various languages, one can hear it rise and fill the whole congregation. For me it is a wonderful Pentecost experience. Without being able to understand the words of the other languages, one knows what everyone else is saying. The event becomes a common prayer for all participants. All are speaking in their own native languages, yet all are a part of what the others are praying. The Babel of many languages is overcome in the prayer Jesus taught us to pray. God's reconciling power is among us.

The Lord's Prayer begins by honoring the Holy name. It begins in worship, in devotion to God, in believing and addressing God. It begins in the conviction that all of life is a matter of addressing God. Then it calls on God to bring God's kingdom into being on earth. We all understand that the coming kingdom is one of peace. It certainly isn't a kingdom of violence. Indeed it is unthinkable that Jesus would be praying for a kingdom of violence. The problem Jesus faced was that the authorities thought he was a violent king, so they executed him. But he was not a violent king. He was a king of peace, and he didn't respond violently to their judgments against him. When we pray, "Thy Kingdom come," we are calling for peace on earth.

The prayer goes on to ask that each and every one of us have our daily bread. This petition points to the economic problems of life. God's will is that all people be fed, that they have sufficient food no matter what their tradition or religion or place of residence. It is God's will that our economies work so that no one is overwhelmed with poverty. At the same time, all Christians know that a prayer for bread includes the breaking of bread in the communion service. It includes the Word of God and the worship of God. Our need for both physical and spiritual nourishment is held together in the prayer for daily bread.

Next we pray for forgiveness, "Forgive us our debts as we forgive our debtors." The heart of healing and reconciliation is forgiveness, and forgiveness is at the very center of the prayer. There can be no peace without forgiveness. True forgiveness is often so difficult that it can come only as a gift from God. We cannot be forgiven without being willing to forgive others.

Jesus is very realistic about the kinds of threats to peace in our lives. We listen to the stories of the awful things that have happened in our lives, the violence we have experienced. Tears come to our eyes as we listen, and we realize how hurtful these experiences have been. Jesus' prayer is, "Lord, deliver us from this evil; lead us not into temptation." Deliver us from violence. You can substitute the word *violence* for the word *evil* and the prayer remains nearly the same.

Finally, the prayer affirms that violence does not have ultimate power over life. Violence will not have the last word. Thine is the kingdom, the kingdom of peace, of power, and of glory forever. We believe that this is Jesus' word for us. The peace churches have a mission to teach the people to pray this prayer, a prayer that all Christians pray, with a rich and deep understanding of its meaning for peace on earth. Then the many languages surrounding us in our common faith in Jesus Christ, who taught us to pray in this way, will remind us that God's will is that there be peace on earth.

41

BUILDING PEACE, HEALING, FORGIVENESS, AND RENEWAL

Fernando Enns (Germany)

LET US MEDITATE ON building peace, healing, forgiveness, and renewal. I don't speak French, but numerous times I've heard the translators use the beautiful phrase, *"artisans de la paix."* To me this phrase sounds like a suggestion to become artists of peacebuilding. And in fact we are together to discover the art of peacebuilding today.

According to the understanding of the peace churches, building peace is not only an issue of ethics but is intrinsic to our understanding of the nature and the mission of the church. What are the implications of such a strong and powerful statement? First of all, it suggests a deep theological grounding when discerning the different aspects of peacebuilding. We need to go back to our confession of faith to be sure about our own identity as peace churches, to be able to communicate to other denominations in the ecumenical family, and also to be faithful and convincing within the societies of which we are a part.

THE ART OF HEALING

The World Council of Churches decided that the theme for world missions conference to be held in 2005 in Greece would be "Come

Holy Spirit, Heal and Reconcile. In Christ called to be Reconciling and Healing Communities." This theme was deliberately chosen in the framework of the Decade to Overcome Violence. And we realize that the first emphasis is not on the mission of the church, but a prayer to the Holy Spirit. Secondly, it is an affirmation that Jesus Christ heals and reconciles. Together with all other Christians, we believe that we are healed and reconciled by the grace of God, not by our works, not by our peacebuilding. We believe that the love revealed in the incarnation, the cross, and the resurrection, is the way that God has healed what was wounded, has reconciled what was broken.

This healing love is granted unconditionally. It liberates us from self-denial, from selfishness, from self-loving, and from self-centeredness. It heals us from the misconception that we have to justify ourselves, that we are going to heal ourselves and heal the world. Once we are realizing the grace in this act of unconditional love, we find ourselves liberated and empowered to undertake the mission of healing ourselves, not primarily as individuals but in communities. I suggest calling it "incarnated healing."

Wherever we face suffering, woundedness, or brokenness, we will discover Christ and—hopefully—the courage and the empowerment to become reconciling and healing communities. This is healing for the HIV/AIDS orphan, healing for the ones who have been discriminated against, healing for the child soldier, healing for the woman who has been raped. I believe that by listening anew to the stories of healing in the New Testament we will realize that Jesus has given his disciples the power to heal and to cast out demons, including the demons of economic injustice and of hatred between religions and ethnic groups.

THE ART OF FORGIVENESS

Let me tell you a story from my context in Germany. Simon Wiesenthal, a Jew who was imprisoned in a concentration camp in Lemberg during the Second World War in Germany, was among those who had to leave the camp every morning to walk to the hospital for the German soldiers and clean the messy place. One morning he was called by one of the nurses, "Hey you, Jew, you come with me." She led him into a dark room where he could hardly see anything. After a while he was able to catch a glimpse of a wounded soldier in the bed who had his head totally covered with a bandage. The nurse left the Jew with the man.

The patient asked straightforwardly, "Are you a Jew?" "Yes," he replied, not knowing what this was all about. "You need to listen," the soldier said. Then he told his story about how one day he was part of burning the houses of Jews after locking them from outside. One Jewish family the soldier had seen jumping out of a window to their death. "You have to forgive me," the soldier cried, "I cannot die unforgiven. You are a Jew. You have to forgive me."

Simon Wiesenthal did not know what to say. On that day he left the room without saying one word. He did not sleep during that night. He discussed it with the other prisoners. The next day he went to see the soldier but he could not find him. The soldier had died that very morning. Many years later, Simon Wiesenthal presented the difficult questions to fellow Jews and Christians: "Did this man die unforgiven?"

Do we become guilty if we cannot speak the word of forgiveness? Helmut Gollwitzer, a Christian theologian, replied that "even if the German could not hear the word of forgiveness from you, the whole Bible tells us to hope for him that he will have heard it from God. Obviously this presupposes that we take seriously the extraordinary opinion of the Bible, that in death all our possibilities come to an end, but not God´s possibilities."

Ernst Simon replied, "Maybe there will come a time in which the descendants of the murderers and the descendants of the murdered will realize, that both murderer and murdered had become victims of a horrible enmeshment of humankind—and especially the German people—acting victims and suffering victims. . ." (Simon Wiensenthal, *Die Sonnenblume,* Eine Erzählung von Schuld und Vergebung. Frankfurt/M, Berlin: Ullstein, 1993).

I believe that the art of forgiveness will grow out of the faith that we have been forgiven by the grace of God, that sinners we are and sinners we remain. This is not a cheap grace. It is a costly grace (cf. Dietrich Bonhoeffer). We know that we ought to forgive whenever possible, for the sake of the other as well as for our own sake. That is the only way to have peace in our heart. But when it comes to violence, forgiveness becomes very costly; sometimes we just will not be able to forgive because to do so seems inhuman.

Forgiveness is not something we can demand from victims of violence, even if the victims are Christians. The victim himself, the victim herself, decides where and when forgiveness is possible. We can only rely on the greater forgiveness of God and pray that this will enable and educate us in the art of forgiveness. This includes the art of forgiveness among ourselves, with other Christians, with people of other faiths, and with all of creation. Forgiveness is a way of breaking the cycle of violence. And since it is so costly we will have to rely on the support of a strong community, especially in those times when we are not able to forgive.

THE GIFT OF RENEWAL

We live in a fallen world. This is the theological explanation for the existence of evil, including violence. God's kingdom has come into the midst of this fallen world to renew, to bring about a new creation. We believe that we, by the work of the Holy Spirit, are part of this new creation even when we experience ourselves as belonging to the fallen world. We belong to the fallen world with all our anger, our fear, our aggression, and our violence. "*Simul justus et peccator*," we say in Latin; at the same time justified and sinners. The only way to live with this dilemma is to hope for continuing renewal through the Holy Spirit, the Spirit of Love—creator, sustainer, and renewer of all relations. To believe in the triune God implies believing in the possibility of renewal of violently broken relations.

This is not something we can perform. This is not an art we can learn. Renewal is a gift of the Holy Spirit that we can pray for, together with others. To believe in this power is, in the end, the only hope there is for this fallen world, its injustice, its poverty, its discrimination, its torture, its abuse, its violence. There will be no peace church without the renewing power of the Spirit.

All theological insights and confessions I believe are meaningless when they do not become relevant to people's lives. We are not worthy to be called a peace church, even a Historic Peace Church, if our witness, our mission, our faith, is not affecting the public arena. I strongly believe that we members of Historic Peace Churches have a responsibility to shape the societies we live in. We will have to learn to defend human rights together with others. We will engage ourselves in interfaith dialogue. We will be ready to take part in political responsibilities. And as we have heard from these stories of African peacemakers, this is already taking place in Africa.

The peace church is a dialoguing church. To get engaged is not an option; it is really an obligation for the peace church. We have something to contribute: the conviction that we will not overcome evil by evil, but by good. As peace churches, we will have to be creative in finding a nonviolent but active third way. Let me end by quoting Musa Dube, who teaches New Testament in Botswana. She says,

> It is now more pressing than ever to proclaim the kingdom of God, the good news and the fullness of life. It is now more than ever that the church needs to proclaim liberty throughout the land, to announce freedom to the slaves, the poor, the women, to orphans, and to insist on the redistribution of wealth to and for all. It is now that total healing needs to become the mission of the church to the world. (Musa W. Dube, "Fülle des Lebens im Zeitalter von HIV/Aids und wirtschaftlicher Globalisierung: Eine Herausforderung an die Mission der Kirchen," in *Öku-menische Rundschau* 4, Frankfurt/M: Lembeck, 2004, 459-476)

Sisters and brothers, we should not be afraid, because we will find out that we are not alone on this journey of hope. There are many others walking with us. It is really an ecumenical journey. I pray that God will bless us on this journey with the arts of peacebuilding: healing, forgiveness, and renewal.

42

THE BIBLICAL VIEW OF PEACE, WEALTH, AND POVERTY

Abraham Wuta Tizhe (Nigeria)

FROM A BIBLICAL PERSPECTIVE, addressing the problem of wealth and poverty is essential to achieving peace. God said that everything he created in the beginning was good (Gen 1:25). Being good includes the human condition of lacking nothing. God has told Israel that there will be no poor among them (Deut. 15:2, 4, 7, 11). Why are there poor people in Africa, especially among believers? Since there are so many Christians in the world, couldn't they share their wealth with the poor in Africa?

In the Old Testament the king was to protect the poor from exploitation by the rich. However, Samuel told the Israelites that they should not have a king, because the king would make them poor (1 Sam 8:10-12). The prophet Elijah condemned King Ahab for killing Naboth and stealing his vineyard (1 Kings 21). The prophet Zechariah told Israel that the result of their oppressing the poor would be exile (Zech. 7:8-14). The Psalmist pleads on behalf of the poor (Ps. 41:1; 82:3-4). The whole message of the prophet Amos was in opposition to forcing people into poverty.

The good news is defined for all by what it means to the poor (James 2:1-7). What is the message of Christians around the world to the poor? Since most people in the northern hemisphere are rich, they must use their riches in bringing peace to the conflicts in Africa. What Africa needs now is not lip service and eye service, but action—peace through material assistance.

Jesus brought peace into the world, as we read from Isaiah 9:6-7. He brought justice to the poor. Jesus himself was preaching the good news of peace (Acts 10:36). In the peace he was preaching he healed many that were oppressed (Acts 10:28). Peace in Africa must be practical. The master Jesus left peace with his disciples (John 14:27). But today instead of continuing with the gospel of peace, Christians are busy manufacturing weapons of mass destruction. The peace taught by Jesus has received little attention, while billions of dollars are spent year by year on its counterpart.

As a principle of sharing peace, Jesus told the rich young ruler to go, sell what he had and give to the poor, for his treasure was in heaven (Matt. 19:21, Mark 10:21). Can Christians follow Jesus while selling firearms to bring peace into Africa? Here I believe Jesus was telling wealthy Christians, "Go, sell what you have, and give it to the HIV/AIDS pandemic people, so that they can buy anti-retroviral therapy tablets with it!"

If the God of peace rules in our hearts (Col. 3:15), what prevents us from assisting the hungry, thirst-stricken nations rather than spending it on nuclear weapons? The northern hemisphere has been selling firearms to Africa instead of providing the means for poverty alleviation. Can a Christian business person or scientist be involved in either manufacturing firearms or selling them to the conflicted and warring regions of Africa?

Paul says Christians should pursue what makes for peace and not what makes for conflict and war (Rom. 16:20). I see Christians of the northern hemisphere pursuing the spacecraft Mercury, Mars, and DNA research when they are able to pursue peace in Africa by providing resources for food, water, habitat. and HIV/AIDS pandemic. This would abate conflicts and wars in Africa. Jesus said, "Blessed are the peacemakers" (Matt. 5:9). Peace and righteousness are what God wants (Ps. 85:10; Heb. 7:2). The law of Jesus is to love your enemies and pray for them (Matt. 5:44). Jesus did not say, "Go and destroy your enemies and support the warring nations so that you can easily sell your firearms.

To make peace theology relevant to the challenges of conflicts and wars in Africa. we must engage in the works of faith, love, service, patience. We must keep God's commandments. We must also emulate the pacifists who have visualized peace in terms of peoplehood through the preaching of universal love. They have always unconditionally opposed and renounced international violence of any type and refused on the basis of religious, humanitarian, philosophical, and social justice principles to participate in or support conflicts and wars for any reason.

From whatever vantage point, we might address the theology of making peace relevant to the conflicts and wars in Africa, Christ's method is the ultimate way. A product of its colonial past, Africa is still today a ground for showing Christian love; especially as it is still stricken with hunger, bound in poverty, and sick with the HIV/AIDS pandemic. We must not preach peace for eye service. Rather peace to Africa is an action of compassion like that on the Jericho Road. May the good Lord bless us to really turn to ourselves inwardly and help with making peace theology relevant to the conflicts and wars in Africa.

43

THE WAY AHEAD

Toma Ragnjiya (Nigeria)

MY FOCUS IS MUSLIM-CHRISTIAN RELATIONSHIPS in Nigeria. The relationship between Muslims and Christians in northern Nigeria seems impossible to many, even among the Christian folk. During an ecumenical conference in 2003, I met somebody who said that the text says you should be as wise as a serpent. Then he said he would not rush but would be as harmless as a dove. This person is a minister, someone in the church. So the conference encouraged me and helped me to be more committed to establishing a relationship of trust between Muslims and Christians.

There are Muslim leaders willing to have dialogue. However, such dialogue often is on an intellectual level. What I am concerned about is the grassroots level, where you really talk with the victims of violence. My objective is to be able to talk not just as an academic exercise in which we speak of philosophical questions and then leave them. I want a simple language that people can understand.

Fortunately, in Nigeria in any conflict that has to do with religion, the federal government usually calls together the Islamic Council and the Christian Association of Nigeria to pose this question, "What do we do?" Meetings like the Watu Wa Amani conference are good opportunities we should exploit. I see a need to work with the community leaders, religious leaders, and government agencies.

We should be concerned about our people who are coming to the church, especially the sixty percent of our congregations who are youth. They are the triggers. They are the people who can be motivated, can be engaged or involved in conflicts and violence. They are unemployed people who can be set off by any small thing. It is just a matter of touching a button, and they will go into conflict. In African culture you are supposed to respect your elders, but you have to approach the youth before a crisis arises. By the time conflict has escalated to a crisis stage, no amount of theology can prevent these young people from acting.

Religious leaders should also try to monitor rumors. These conflicts don't happen just in one day, so we should not ignore what we are hearing in common conversation in the market or on the bus. Leaders should listen to the movement, to what is going on, and start working on it. Conflict in Nigeria can be controlled, because it rises and lasts for no more than three days. It has never gone beyond that. Then the government uses its own methods of sending the military or police to stop it by force. When tension is low is the time for us as peacemakers to bring people together and talk about what they desire for the future. Ask them what kind of future they want to leave. If you are able to stop the fighting and then do nothing beyond that, you're just giving them the opportunity to go on and plan to attack each other again.

As people seeking peace, what we should do, when the tension is a bit low, is to pick out some leaders and talk about the violence. Don't wait until it breaks into conflict again. Talk about the kind of future we want to leave. What legacy are we leaving to our children? That is the way ahead.

AFTERWORD:
WHAT HAPPENED HERE?

Deenabandhu Manchala (India)

THE WATU WA AMANI CONFERENCE proved to be a very enriching and challenging experience of listening not only to stories of violence but also to stories of how, despite all the difficulties, communities of Christians are trying to overcome violence in their own way. I thank God for that. Despite the fact that the conference left us with several questions, I am encouraged to believe that the churches can make a difference in the overwhelming culture of violence in this world and especially in Africa today.

I coordinate the work of theological reflection on peace, with several persons, including the Mennonite coordinator for the Decade to Overcome Violence, who take care of other responsibilities related to seeking peace. From the perspective of my role, I saw the Watu Wa Amani discussion as a distinct, creative contribution to the Decade to Overcome Violence process, for other churches can learn from what the churches in Africa have to say about overcoming violence.

Having said that, I want to make five observations. These are based on three premises.

One premise is that I speak as a person from the World Council of Churches working on the Decade to Overcome Violence. I want to reflect with you on how this contribution is valuable and is going to be useful for the whole decade process.

A second premise is that I want to reflect on this experience in particular as a contextual theologian from the south. Let me explain what I mean by "contextual theologian." I have studied systematic theology, but as my vocation I have taken up theology based on the context and experience of the marginalized communities in India, the social outcasts. So one of the things that we affirm and advocate is the inductive way of doing theology—that is, beginning with a theological analysis of the context and experience out of which we understand and interpret what the faith and the Scriptures have to tell us.

My third premise is that I want to look at this experience by sharing our common legacy as Christians from the south—the legacy of missionary history, the legacy of colonialism, and the legacy of a diversity of denominations back home in India.

A recurrent assertion in this volume is the affirmation that love and peace are intrinsic to the nature and purpose of the church. This, for me, is a crucial statement that comes from these discussions.

The World Council of Churches has been working on ecclesiology—that is, the doctrine of the church—for a long time. This effort has been directed towards understanding the mission of the church, the purpose of the church, and the nature of the church in the constantly changing world throughout the history of the World Council of Churches. An important hallmark of this ongoing study has been the effort of the ecclesiology and ethics study program to bring together a description of the purpose of the church. One conclusion highlighted by the study is that the vocation of the church is the doctrine that not only validates the purpose of the church but also determines the nature of the church. In other words, ethics is central in the affirmation of faith as well as in the practice of the faith.

In addition to this, the study also points out that if the church is not involved in the mission of God, it is not a church at all. It says that the church makes present through its form and functions the promise of God's reign in the world. At the same time, the church makes present the promise that has been given to us in Jesus Christ.

These issues are not easily resolved. There are many questions, debates, and controversies around the whole idea of the nature and purpose of the church. They continue to dominate the agenda of the ecumenical movement, especially in Faith and Order, because the various churches have different notions of church, the being of the church, and the purpose of the church. The WCC hopes that it will soon be able to make a convergence statement about this range of issues.

Thus my first observation is that what I have heard in the stories presented here is that we are affirming and upholding the ethical issue of the value of peace as a reason for the church. I believe that the Decade to Overcome Violence presents a new opportunity for the churches to come together and to work together. In the past, the ecumenical movement has been seeking Christian unity by finding a convergence of understanding regarding certain doctrines, such as baptism, apostolic faith, eucharist, ministry, and other doctrines. We have been trying to sort out these differences and come to a common understanding, so that we can stay together and work together. The Watu Wa Amani gathering has tremendous ecumenical significance because of our focus on the vocation of overcoming violence and building peace. Therefore, I want to stress this particular affirmation voiced again and again in these stories.

One further point needs to be made before moving to the next observation. When ethics are discussed, I often say that somehow the emphasis on ethics is not so prominent in the way Christians understand the meaning and implications of the salvation granted to the world in Jesus Christ. The reason for this lack of ethical emphasis is that our notions of salvation are so centered around the cross event that we tend to give a kind of mystical, very spiritual significance to the cross. However, we have often failed to recognize the salvific significance in Jesus' life, his incarnation, his message, his hard choices, the options he chose, his prophetic actions, and all that led him to the cross.

I hope that I am making myself clear. We are so centered upon, and have focused so much upon the event of the cross—the violent act of Jesus dying for the salvation of humankind—that the cross is used as a kind of legitimization of the violence needed for salvation. But we have not focused so much our attention on the things that preceded the cross. We need to reclaim the soteriological, or the salvific, significance in the totality of Jesus' life, death, and resurrection. This is crucial but is certainly not a very attractive thing for many Christians who believe that a passive hope or a passive belief in Jesus Christ makes things all right in this world.

The second observation I would like to offer is this: We have upheld the affirmation of life as a key element of our faith. By upholding peace or in committing ourselves to a vocation of peace, we are affirming life. Because we want to overcome violence, we want to build peace so that the gift of life that God has given to each one of us and to this world is sustained, valued, and protected. Therefore we commit ourselves to upholding the sanctity, dignity, and worth of all forms of life. The vocation of peace is not just a humanitarian service; it is a spiritual vocation, a vocation of affirming the life that God has created.

The option to overcome violence is an option for life. Through this option we affirm our faith in the God of life. And through this option we call upon the churches to set aside their differences and work together for the sake of life. This commitment to life is what makes us willing to trespass our ecclesiastical boundaries and join hands with people of other faiths, people of no faiths, and peoples' movements. For the sake of life we call upon all people of good will, all who are pro-life, to come and work for peace.

In Christian communities there is sometimes ambiguity when we talk about life, because we have become accustomed to seeing life or understanding life in a way that is too limited. Some Christians look at life on earth as a mere illusion, or mostly in terms of the life of the soul. Some consider the life of the Christian as the life of our own little communities, without really caring for the life of the rest of the world. When we are working for peace, we are committing ourselves to the totality of life and the integrity of creation.

My third observation is that the Decade to Overcome Violence has helped the churches to look at violence and to understand it. Violence is not just a behavioral trait that some people and some communities have, something that we need to help them overcome. The Decade has helped us to unmask the faces of the perpetrators of violence and to discern the implications of power behind violence. We would all agree that violence is not just a behavioral trait but an instrument of power in the hands of those who have the power to subjugate, to terrorize, to dominate, to exploit, and also to disempower people.

Violence is an instrument of power. Therefore, when we are committing ourselves to the task of building peace, which is our vocation, this must include political activism. Peace is a political issue. So when bad politics spoil the chances for peace, it is necessary for us to play good politics for the sake of peace. Political activism is an important element in our task of building peace.

How do we do this? How do we strengthen the voices of those struggling for justice, struggling to reveal the hidden intentions of the perpetrators of violence and injustice in the world today? It is important to forgive one another and to be reconciled, but I think it is equally important for us in the spirit of the gospel to enable people to seek forgiveness. This is a prophetic role that we must keep in mind.

If you take a look at many of the parables of Jesus and many of his actions, especially in the synoptic gospels, you will find that the message of the kingdom is often addressed to the privileged and the powerful. In that sense it becomes good news to the poor. The man with two coats is asked to give one away. The older son is asked not to grumble when the younger son is received back into the fold. Those who come in the morning are asked not to complain when those who come in the evening receive the same wages. The rich young ruler is asked to give up all his riches, make himself totally vulnerable, and share with the others. We as churches need to maintain this prophetic role so our efforts as people of peace maintain their distinctive edge as a Christian response.

We have been discussing terrorism and counter-terrorism as a problem to be overcome. At the same time, it is important for us to deal with the causes of terrorism, the clandestine forms of terrorism that disempower our people in so many ways.

As people from the south, we carry with us the history of colonialism by which our continents and our countries were plundered. The newer forms of colonialism continue to disempower our communities: the legitimate trade, the multinational corporations, the debt, the economic globalization, and increasing poverty. How do we express peace toward the structures which annihilate millions of people in many parts of the world? In my country, India, there are not many very active violent conflicts except in one or two places. But my country is the home of nearly 300 million hungry people. For me that is a worse form of violence than any other visible form of violence, whether bombs or anything else. This is structural injustice, structural violence. How do I as a Christian respond to the structural violence that causes such destruction and death in the lives of many communities in the world?

My fourth observation is the importance of interfaith dialogue and working with people of other faiths for the cause of peace. The vocation of peacebuilding calls us not only to set aside our differences but also to cross the boundaries of our ecclesiastical traditions for the sake of life, for the sake of peace. That trespassing is not an offensive trespassing but is rather seeking the hand of friendship with the other. I say this because in India, where Christians are about a 2.5 percent minority, for us to take upon ourselves any of these issues is impossible. We are very small in number and economically disempowered. Not only that, we are engaged not just in a Christian issue, but in a people's issue, in a world issue: peace. We cannot build peace without the partnership of others. This is where interfaith dialogue becomes an important element, something that we need to continue to pursue and affirm.

As my fifth and final observation, I want to commend this inductive way of doing theology. We have analyzed our own situations of violence and conflict, and we have looked at the world that is in front of us through our own eyes. Now we can begin to look at the Scriptures and our theologies on the basis of the experience that we have had. The point is that we must search within our own experience, within our cultural traditions, for ways by which community-based or people-based peacemaking is possible and successful. This is exactly what the Decade to Overcome Violence is all about. It tries to identify people-based initiatives for building peace, so that we can uphold hope amid turmoil. The Decade to Overcome Violence process looks to Africa and to the Historic Peace Churches in Africa for leadership and inspiration.

THE DECADE TO OVERCOME VIOLENCE

Donald Miller (USA)

THE DECADE TO OVERCOME VIOLENCE (DOV)—Churches Seeking Reconciliation and Peace (2001-2010) was adopted by the World Council of Churches (WCC) at its Eighth General Assembly held in Harare, Zimbabwe, in 1998. It builds on the Program to Overcome Violence (POV) adopted by the Central Committee of the WCC at a meeting in South Africa in 1994 shortly before apartheid was voted out of power there. It also parallels the United Nations Decade for a Culture of Peace and Nonviolence for the Children of the World.

The setting in Harare was the last day of the General Assembly, a day in which all official business had been completed and any new business was out of order. Many participants at Harare had urged the extension of the Program to Overcome Violence. However the motion never came to the floor of the assembly for a vote. On the last day, as the Assembly was ready to adjourn, a young Mennonite pastor and scholar named Fernando Enns stood and in a dramatic statement declared that many at the assembly were in favor of extending the Program to Overcome Violence. Therefore he moved the adoption of the Decade. The chair hesitated, not sure how to handle the motion. He turned to his parliamentarian, who quickly said, "Vote on it." The chairperson put the question to a vote, and it passed overwhelmingly.

Immediately the WCC invited churches around the world to find their own ways to participate in the Decade. Violence takes different forms in different places: tribal, ethnic, street, domestic, against women, revolutionary, terrorist, international, and others. Churches were asked to find ways of addressing issues of violence in their own setting. The Historic Peace Churches were specifically asked to share their own experience in addressing these issues. The Friends, the Mennonites, and the Church of the Brethren have often been referred to as the Historic Peace Churches (HPC). Although many churches are deeply committed to a mission of peacemaking, the HPC are widely recognized throughout their history to have taken a more radical stance in resisting violence as a method of solving problems. They are committed to nonviolence, reconciliation, education, and service as a way of opening pathways to peace and they identify this stance as an essential mark of the church.

The WCC has regularly addressed the problems of warfare and violence since its founding in 1948 in Amsterdam, when it declared that all war is sin. During the Cold War, the churches in the World Council addressed the problem of weapons of mass destruction, and they turned to the HPC for counsel. Between 1955 and 1962 the meetings between representatives from both the HPC and other churches to debate the issues of war and violence were known as the Puidoux Conferences. Those discussions had a significant influence on the ecumenical movement and in some cases on wider political processes.

At the Fourth General Assembly of the World Council of Churches in Upsala in 1968, Wilmer Cooper of the Friends offered a resolution in response to the recent assassination of Martin Luther King Jr. This resolution was adopted and became the basis for the Program to Combat Racism (PCR). Perhaps the greatest impact of PCR was its influence in the defeat of apartheid in South Africa. Bishop Tutu and Nelson Mandela both give considerable credit to the PCR as a factor in the overcoming of apartheid.

When the Central Committee of the WCC met in South Africa in January 1994, the air was electric with expectation. Elections were only a few weeks away—and everyone expected apartheid to be voted out of power, even though much violence continued. At the opening worship service, Methodist Bishop Stanley Mogoba declared that at the time of such an historic event, the WCC should initiate a program to combat violence. The suggestion seemed to fall on deaf ears. A member of the Church of the Brethren introduced a resolution for a Program to Combat Violence, but it was not accepted. He then appealed to WCC General Secretary Konrad Raiser, who suggested that such a program could be initiated without additional expense or additional staff. It could become an emphasis rather than a new program, and it could bring together the various efforts of the WCC to address the question of violence. Rephrased as the Program to Overcome Violence, the resolution was unanimously accepted by the Central Committee. The success of this program led to the adoption of the Decade to Overcome Violence at the WCC's Eighth General Assembly in Zimbabwe, in 1998, as noted above.

The WCC describes The Decade in this way:

> The Decade to Overcome Violence (2001-2010), churches seeking reconciliation and peace, calls churches, ecumenical organizations and all people of good will—to work together at all levels (local, regional, global) with communities, secular movements, people of all living faiths for peace, justice, and reconciliation.
>
> It calls us to walk with those oppressed by violence, and act in solidarity with those struggling for justice, peace, and integrity of creation.
>
> It calls us to repent for our complicity in violence, and to engage in theological reflection to overcome the spirit, logic, and practice of violence.

As an initiative of the World Council of Churches, the Decade is a global movement. It attempts to strengthen existing peace networks as well as inspire the creation of new ones.

The Decade to Overcome Violence is a challenge to churches around the world to address the many ways in which violence degrades human life. The church is a sign of God's hope in a world often controlled by despair. The calling of the churches is to contribute to a culture of peace. In the words of Samuel Kobia, the General Secretary of the World Council of Churches, "We are confident that the current efforts under way (Watu Wa Amani) have the capacity and potential to engender fruitful dialogue and to empower the voices of the HPC beyond Europe and North America for the benefit of the ecumenical family as it engages in a decade-long journey of overcoming violence."

MESSAGE TO ALL CHURCHES FROM WATU WA AMANI—PEOPLE OF PEACE, LIMURU / NAIROBI, KENYA, AUGUST 2004

TO ALL THOSE WHO ARE WITH US in the journey of hope to overcome violence:

(1) We, representatives of Historic Peace Churches (Church of the Brethren, Friends, and Mennonites/Brethren in Christ), and distinguished ecumenical guests from the National Council of Churches in Kenya, the Association of Evangelicals in Africa and the World Council of Churches are gathered in Limuru, Kenya, to continue the conversation on peace theology and peacebuilding within the framework of the ecumenical *Decade to Overcome Violence 2001-2010—Churches seeking Reconciliation and Peace.* We are grateful for the hospitality that we have experienced from the Kenyan Friends and the Brackenhurst Baptist International Conference Center.

(2) This conference is a continuation of the process that started in 2001 in Bienenberg, Switzerland (the proceedings of which are available in *Seeking Cultures of Peace: A Peace Church Conversation*, edited by Fernando Enns, Scott Holland, Ann Riggs, and published by Cascadia Publishing House, copublished with WCC and Herald Press, 2004). During that conference it became clear that future conversations about peace theology and practice need to take into account much more the perspectives of people from the southern hemisphere.

This has brought us to Kenya, the second international conference of the HPC. The majority of nearly 100 participants are peace-educators, peace-trainers and peace-theologians from different countries in Africa.

(3) WATU WA AMANI has provided us with the opportunity to address the theological, institutional, and praxis issues that arise in the African context from the perspective of Historic Peace Churches. The tradition of these churches provides us with an identity that carries the message of love for the neighbor and the enemy, not only being part of our ethics, but being intrinsic to our understanding of the very nature and mission of the church, rooted in the nonviolent self-giving love of Christ. With other Christians in the ecumenical family we listen to our call to be ambassadors of reconciliation (2 Cor. 5).

(4) We have told and listened to painful stories from Africa, stories soaked with terrible experiences of violence (Kenya, D. R. Congo, Burkina Faso, Burundi, Rwanda, the Great Lakes Region, Nigeria, Ethiopia, Somalia, Sudan, and Zimbabwe). We have shared different analyses and have searched for theological interpretations. It is the fallen world that we live in and that we are a part of. The threats to peace in this continent are manyfold: frequent misuse of religion by political as well as religious leaders; ethnic and religious plurality misused for political interests; human dignity violated in many ways (especially against women); economic imbalance, poverty, and HIV/AIDS.

(5) This is not the way of the peace churches. We believe—together with all other Christians—that we are healed and reconciled by the grace of God. We believe that the love that is revealed in the incarnation, the cross, and the resurrection is the way God has healed what is wounded and reconciled what was broken. This healing love is given to us unconditionally. It liberates us from self-denial, from selfishness, from self-love and self-centeredness. Therefore we participate in God's shalom, which creates right relations: with our creator, between each other, with all of creation. This peace is spiritual and social, interactive and interdependent ("a person becomes a person through persons"). We feel liberated and empowered to a mission of peacebuilding-processes in prevention, nonviolent conflict transformation, and the art of healing. The gift of renewal by the Holy Spirit leads us to search for the "third way": active nonviolence.

(6) Amid widespread despair and trauma, we Historic Peace Churches in Africa are living our faith by ministries of prayer, by

breaking the silence, by showing our presence in places of conflict, by getting in direct contact with armed groups, by initiating dialogues between governments and opposition groups when public space is closed for all other non-governmental organizations, and by facing the tension between Christian and Muslim communities. We try to listen and tell the stories from the victim's perspectives and to provide alternative perspectives to all sides of a conflict by spreading information. We work in peace and justice committees, we are providing trauma-healing centers, we are training our pastors in nonviolent conflict transformation and healing skills for victims and relatives. We are developing seminars on political situations, special ministries to women, and peacebuilding youth programs. We build networks with other churches and organizations as we seek voices of support from outside one country.

(7) But further exploration is needed: our role in the public sphere, "seeking the welfare of the city" (Jer. 29); the relation of identity and diversity, confession and tolerance, to value uniqueness and identity as well as plurality; the spiritual and theological resources in our faith as well as in the faith of others for peacebuilding; indigenous African peacemaking practices; how to relate to fundamentalism of any sort (including terrorism and counter-terrorism); a restorative/transformative conception of justice, reconciliation processes that include restitution.

Our journey of hope continues. We believe there is hope for healing, reconciliation, and renewal in Africa. We believe there is hope for peace in Africa. We invite all people of goodwill to join in becoming what we are called to be: WATU WA AMANI.

CONFERENCE PARTICIPANTS

WATU WA AMANI, AUGUST 8-14, 2004, NAIROBI, KENYA

Samson Ababu
Kenya
Friends

Dr. Agnes Abuom
Kenya
WCC

Maurice O. Anyanga
Kenya
Mennonite

Jean Claude Balinda
Kenya
Friends

Million Belete
Ethiopia
Meserete

Melissa Bennett
USA
Brethren

Salamatu Joel Billi
Nigeria
EYN

Rejoice R. Birma
Nigeria
EYN

Lucas Bishop
USA
Mennonite

Mkoko Boseka
Congo
Friends

Adamu Buba
Nigeria
EYN

David Bucura
Rwanda
Friends

Patrick Bugu
Nigeria
EYN

Ayuba Bulus
Nigeria
EYN

Benjamin Chawachi
Tanzania
Mennonite

Mutah Abba Chibok
Nigeria
EYN

Abdias Coulibaly
Burkina Faso
Mennonite

Ed Cundiff
USA

Kubili David
Nigeria
EYN

Bitrus V. Z. Debki
Nigeria
EYN

Safiya O. Doma
Nigeria
EYN

Pathisiwe Dube
Zimbabwe
Mennonite

Fernando Enns
Germany
Mennonite

Lon Fendall
USA
Friends

Matthew Abdullahi Gali
Nigeria
EYN

Tefera Gonfa
Ethiopia
Meserete

Filibus Gwama
Nigeria
EYN

Ahmed Haile
Kenya
Mennonite

Mary Madu Hamman
Nigeria
EYN

Bob Herr
USA
Mennonite

Scott Holland
USA
Brethren

Dean Johnson
USA
Brethren

Benjamin Kabuya
Congo
Mennonite

Fanta B. Kajal
Nigeria
EYN

Ramazani Kakozi
Congo
Friends

Komuesa Kalunga
Congo
Mennonite

Merv Keeney
USA
Brethren

Bruce Khumalo
Zimbabwe
Mennonite

Dieudonne Kibinakanwa
Burundi
Friends

Malesi Elizabeth Kinaro
Kenya
Friends

Pascal Tshisola Kulungu
Congo
Mennonite

Peter Kwaji
Nigeria
EYN

Florence Machayo
Kenya
Friends

Aminu G. Madani
Nigeria
EYN

Deenabandhu Manchala
India
WCC

Steven W. Mang'ana
Tanzania
Mennonite

Suzan Mark
Nigeria
EYN

Hezron Cotts Masitsa
Kenya
Friends

Wendy Matheny
USA
Brethren

Givule Matungulu Floribert
Congo
Mennonite

Kennedy Kerreh Mayabi
Kenya
Friends

Arthur McFarlane
USA
Mennonite

Patricia McFarlane
USA
Mennonite

Lotan Migaliza
Kenya
Friends

Harold Miller
USA
Mennonite

Donald Miller
USA
Brethren

Nellie Mlotshwa
Zimbabwe
Mennonite

Esther Mombo
Kenya
Friends

Cathy Mputu
Congo
Mennonite

John Afanda Muhanj
Kenya
Friends

Kelbessa Muleta
Ethiopia
Meserete

Norah Musundi
Kenya
Friends

Elie Nahimana
Burundi
Friends

Philippe Nakuwundi
Burundi
Friends

Charles Ndegwa
Kenya
Mennonite\

Mbode Ndirmbita
Nigeria
EYN

Albert Ndlovu
Zimbabwe
Mennonite

Joel Ndlovu
Zimbabwe
Mennonite

Patson Netha
Zimbabwe
Association of
Evangelicals

David Niyonzima
Burundi
Friends

Cecile Nyiramana
Rwanda
Friends

Misakabu Pascal Nzal
Congo
Mennonite

Elizabeth Osir
Kenya
Mennonite

Toma Ragnjiya
Nigeria
EYN

Ben Richmond
USA
Friends

Ann Riggs
USA
Friends

Mary Robert
Nigeria
EYN

Janet Scott
England
Friends

Samuel B. Shinggu
Nigeria
EYN

Oliver Kisaka Simiyu
Kenya
Friends

Marcellin Sizeli
Rwanda
Friends

Aletha Stahl
USA
Mennonite

Abraham Wuta Tizhe
Nigeria
EYN

Siaka Traore
Burkina Faso
Mennonite

Janina Traxler
USA

Cathrine J. Tumba
Nigeria

Benjamin Wafulah
Kenya

Paulus Widjaja
Indonesia
Mennonite

Dawn Ottoni Wilhelm
USA
Brethren

Tsegaye Wodajo
Ethiopia
Meserete

Eric Mukambu Ya'
Namwisi
Congo
Mennonite

David Zarembka
USA
Friends

Judy Zimmerman-
Herr
USA
Mennonite

WATU WA AMANI: PEOPLE OF PEACE

Making peace theology relevant to the challenges of conflicts in Africa

**A Conference of the Historic Peace Churches in Africa
Brackenhurst International Conference Center
Limuru/Nairobi, Kenya
August 8 - 14, 2004**

SUNDAY, AUGUST 8

Welcome and greetings
  Lotan Migaliza
  Agnes Abuom
  Patson Netha
  Donald Miller
Evening worship led by the Kenyan Friends
  Speaker: Oliver Kisaka Simiyu

MONDAY, AUGUST 9

Theme: Who Are We? The heritage of the originating churches and the heritage of the African churches.

  Presiding: Comoderator Agnes Abuom
  Morning Prayer
  Statement of the theme: Fernando Enns
  Brethren Heritage: Scott Holland and Filibus Gwama
  Mennonite Heritage: Paulus Widjaja and Komuesa Kalunga

Friends Heritage: Ann Riggs and Malesi Elizabeth Kinaro
Discussion in small groups
Evening worship led by Brethren in Christ Church
   in Zimbabwe
     Speaker: Bruce Khumalo

TUESDAY, AUGUST 10

Theme: Threats to Peace. What are the multiple threats that stand in the way of peace in Africa?

Presiding: Comoderator Donald Miller
Morning Prayer
Statement of Theme: Donald Miller
Storyteller Cathy Mputu from the Congo
Storyteller Albert Ndlovu from Zimbabwe
Storyteller Harold Miller about Sudan
Storyteller Pascal Kulungu from the Congo
Theological paper by Toma Ragnjiya
Theological Panel
   Nellie Mlotshwa
   Esther Mombo
   Fernando Enns
   Patrick Bugu
Discussion in small groups
Evening worship led by EYN in Nigeria
   Speaker: Abraham Wuta Tizhe

WEDNESDAY, APRIL 11

Theme: Christian Faithfulness and the Common Good. What does Christian faithfulness contribute to the wellbeing of multicultural communities?

Presiding: Comoderator Agnes Abuom
Morning Prayer
Statement of Theme: Agnes Abuom
Storyteller Matthew Abdulllahi Gali from Nigeria
Storyteller Adamu Buba from Nigeria
Storyteller Bitrus Debki from from Nigeria
Storyteller Ramazani Kakozi from the Congo
Theological paper by Ahmed Haile
Theological comment by Deenabandhu Manchala
Theological Panel of Mlotshwa, Mombo, Enns, Bugu
Discussion in small groups

Evening worship led by Friends from the Great Lakes
Speaker: Mkoko Boseka

THUSDAY, AUGUST 12

Theme: Building Peace. What are the possibilities for and evidence of healing, forgiveness and renewal?

Presiding: Comoderator Donald Miller
Morning Prayer
Statement of the theme: Fernando Enns
Statement of appreciation by Comoderator Agnes Abuom
Storyteller Benjamin Chiwachi from Tanzania
Storyteller Nora Musundi from Kenya
Storyteller Siaka Traore from Burkina Faso
Storyteller Nyiramana from Rwanda
Storyteller Million Belete from Ethiopia
Theological paper by David Niyonzima
Theological Panel of Mlotshwa, Mombo, Enns, Bugu
Discussion in small groups
Evening worship led by Mennonites
Speaker: Steven Mang'ana from Tanzania

FRIDAY, AUGUST 13

Theme: Where Do We Go from Here? What do we take back to our home communities?

Presiding: Fernando Enns
Morning Prayer
Statement of theme: Donald Miller
Denominational caucuses: What do these discussions mean in our context?
Plenary session: Reports from the denominational caucuses
Response by ecumenical guests
Statements of appreciation to presenters, on site managers, translators, and camera people
Evening worship led by EYN from Nigeria
Speaker: Ayuba Bulus

SATURDAY, AUGUST 14

Farewell and departure

The Index

The Contributors

Dr. Agnes Regina Murei Abuom is Vice President of the World Conference of Religions for Peace. Formerly the Africa President for the World Council of Churches (WCC), as of 2006 she is a member of the WCC Executive Committee. She is also Executive Director of TAABCO Research and Development Consultants. Dr. Abuom's specialties are economic justice and peace and reconciliation. She resides in Kenya, is a lay member of the Anglican Church, and served as Co-moderator of the Watu Wa Amani conference.

Million Belete attended the Watu Wa Amani conference as a representative of the Meserete Kristos Church, of which he was the first chairperson. He was active in the Mennonite World Conference from 1965 to 1978 and was president for one term. For some time he was involved with the Africa Mennonite and Brethren in Christ Fellowship. For a number of years he was the United Bible Societies Regional Secretary for Africa. He is now retired and living in Ethiopia.

Salamatu Joel Billi is an active woman in the Ekklesiyar Yan'uwa a Nigeria (EYN), Church of the Brethren in Nigeria.

Mkoko Boseka is the legal representative of Communaute des Eglises Evangeliques des Amis au Congo (CEEACO), meaning Community of Evangelical Churches of the Friends in the Congo. He resides in the village of Abeka, the region of Fizi, the South Kivu Province of the Democratic Republic of the Congo (DRC). This is the location of the headquarters of the yearly meeting of CEEACO.

Adamu Buba is an evangelist for the EYN (Church of the Brethren in Nigeria). He was formerly Chief of Police in the city of Maiduguri in Borno State of northeastern Nigeria. For thirty-eight years he was a Muslim, then he converted to Christianity in 1999.

Bitrus V. Z. Debki come from the Kamwe (Higgi) people of northeastern Nigeria. For over six years he has served as a pastor of the Ekklesiyar Yan'uwa a Nigeria (EYN, Church of the Brethren in Nigeria).

Dr. Fernando Enns is Professor of Theology and Director of the Institute for Peace Church Theology at the University of Hamburg in Germany. He is a pastor in the German Mennonite Church and vice-chairperson of the Association of Mennonite Congregations in Germany. Since 1998 he has been a member of the Central Committee of the World Council of Churches. He was instrumental in the WCC's action to adopt the current Decade to Overcome Violence at the Eighth WCC World Assembly in Harare, Zimbabwe in 1998, and he serves on the WCC's reference group for the Decade. Dr. Enns holds a Doctor of Theology degree from the University of Heidelberg. He and his wife Renate reside in Hamburg, Germany.

Lon Fendall is the Director of the Center for Global Studies and the Center for Peace and Justice at George Fox University, in Newberg, Oregon. He has served as an academic dean at three colleges and as a staff member for Mark Hatfield, retired Republican Senator from Oregon. He is the author of *Citzenship: A Christian Calling*; and *William Wilberforce: Abolitionist, Politician, and Writer.* He is the co-author of *Unlocking Horns: Forgiveness and Reconciliation in Burundi;* and of *At Home With the Poor.*

Matthew Abdullahi Gali was formerly Pastor of the EYN (Church of the Brethren in Nigeria), church in Kano in northwestesern Nigeria.

Rev. Filibus K. Gwama is from the Zalidiva tribe in Nigeria. He was born in 1944 in the area of Ngoshe, the local government of Gwoza, and the state of Borno. He has been a pastor with the EYN (Church of the Brethren in Nigeria) since 1966 and currently is president of EYN. He received his M.Div. from Bethany Theological Seminary in Richmond, Indiana, USA, in 1995.

Ahmed Ali Haile is a lecturer at Daystar University in Nairobi, Kenya. He has a B.A. degree in Economics from Goshen (Ind.) College; the M.A.P.S. degree from Associated Mennonite Biblical Seminary, Elkhart, Indiana; and the M.P.A. from Indiana State University, Terre Haute, Indiana. He is from Somalia and now resides in Kenya.

Scott Holland teaches peace, public, and cross-cultural theology at Bethany Theological Seminary, in partnership with Earlham School of Religion in Richmond, Indiana. He is contributing editor to *Cross Currents: The Journal of the Association for Religion and Intellectual Life.*

Dean Johnson is Assistant Dean, Director of Plowshares, and Assistant Professor of Peace, Justice, and Conflict Studies at Goshen

(Ind.) College, Goshen, Indiana. He holds an M.Div. from Bethany Theological Seminary and is currently enrolled in doctoral studies at Iliff School of Theology and the University of Denver (Col.). He directed the production of the DVD that documents the 2004 Watu Wa Amani Conference in Nairobi, Kenya.

Ramazoni Kakozi is Director of the Department of Peace for the Community of Evangelical Churches of Friends in the Congo (DRC).

Adolphe Komuesa Kalunga is the national president and legal representative of the Congo Mennonite Community, the largest of three Mennonite denominations in the Congo (DRC). He is a pastor and a theologian who teaches at the Christian University of Kinshasa, Congo.

B. Bruce Khumalo is a Brethren in Christ Church (BICC) pastor in Zimbabwe. He has served in the following ministry involvements: Theological Education by Extension (TEE) instructor and translator; Bible school lecturer and principal; President of all Principals for the African Mennonite colleges; BICC representative to the Mennonite World Conference; Executive Secretary and Treasurer for the Africa Mennonite and BICC Fellowship; national executive of the Evangelical Fellowship of Zimbabwe (EFZ); provincial chair of EFZ; and pastor of a rural BIC church. He was trained in Haggai Institute, Singapore, and Ashland Theological Seminary, Ashland, Ohio. He and his wife Kezineth have five children—four boys and a girl.

Malesi Kinaro is founder of Friends in Peace and Community Development, a Christian peace organization working in western Kenya. Currently she is working as the executive director of a youth empowerment organization in Kenya known as the Uzima Foundation. She is also Coordinator of Friends for Peace and Community Development, which is bringing the Alternatives to Violence Project (AVP) workshops to western Kenya. She is an evangelist/counselor at Ngong Road monthly Meeting of the Nairobi Yearly Meeting of the Friends church in Kenya. She was formerly General Secretary of the Friends World Committee for Consultation—Africa Section.

Rev. Dr. Samuel Kobia, of the Methodist Church in Kenya, was elected General Secretary of the World Council of Churches in August 2003 and took up his new post in January 2004. Earlier in 2003 he served as director and special representative for Africa of the WCC. Before coming to the WCC, Dr. Kobia was general secretary of Kenya's National Council of Churches. From 1978 to 1984 he was WCC executive secretary of Urban Rural Mission and also served as secretary of the WCC Africa Task Force. In 1992 Kobia chaired

Kenya's National Election Monitoring Unit, chaired peace talks for Sudan (1991), helped found the Nairobi Peace Group and the Fellowship of Councils of Churches in Eastern and Southern Africa, was vice-moderator of the Commission of the WCC Programme to Combat Racism (1984-91), chaired the Frontier Internship in Mission International Coordination Committee (1981-85), and helped reorganize the Zimbabwe Christian Council after independence (1980-81).

Pascal Tshisola Kulungu is Director of the Center of Peace Building, Leadership, and Good Governance based in Kinshasa, Democratic Republic of Congo. He is also the Financial Director at Christian University of Kinshasa. In addition, Mr. Kulungu serves as trainer in the area of leadership and good governance, conflict resolution, mediation, and reconciliation. Formerly he served the Congolese Mennonite church as a headmaster and a hospital administrator. He holds a three-year diploma in English and African Culture from Superior Institute in Kikwit; a B.A. in Business Administration and Conflict Studies, and an M.A. in Administrative Leadership and Peace Building from Fresno (Calif.) Pacific University. Mr. Kulungu is married to Therese S. Kulungu. They have six children—four boys and two girls.

Deenabandhu Manchala, a Lutheran pastor and a theologian from India, is Executive Secretary responsible for theological reflection on peace for the Decade to Overcome Violence through the Faith and Order Commission of the World Council of Churches, Geneva, Switzerland.

Steven Mang'ana is a Bishop with the Kanisa la Mennonite Tanzania, Eastern Diocese Dar es Salaam. He holds a diploma in Bible Studies from RBM Bible College, Thika, Kenya, in collaboration with Rosedale Bible College, USA. He has served the Mennonite Church as a deacon, pastor, and as a diocesan secretary.

Donald Miller is an ordained minister of the Church of the Brethren and Emeritus Professor of Christian Education and Ethics at Bethany Theological Seminary in Richmond, Indiana, where he taught for twenty-five years. From 1986-96 he was General Secretary of the General Board of the Church of the Brethren and a member of the Heads of Communion of the National Council of Church of Christ in the U.S. He was also a member of the Central Committee of the World Council of Church 1991-98. He has a Ph.D. in History and Philosophy of Religion from Harvard University, an M.A. from the University of Chicago, and an M.Div. from Bethany Theological Seminary. Miller was co-moderator of the Watu Wa Amani Conference.

Harold Miller served as Mennonite Central Committee's co-representative to Sudan from 1999 to 2005.

Cathy Motuli Mputu is pastor of a Mennonite Brethren parish in the Democratic Republic of the Congo. She is also President of the Association of Women Peacemakers as well as Administrative Secretary for the Mission Department of the Mennonite Brethren Church Conference in Congo. She was born February 6, 1961, in Kinshasa, and she holds a bachelor's degree in Missiology.

Nora Musundi is a member of the Friends Church in Kenya and a peace activist. In the 1990s she formed a distress committee for displaced persons that was supported by the Africa section of the Friends World Committee for Consultation. She organized a national prayer group for women whose peace activities received grants from Sharing the Worlds Resources and UNICEF.

Philippe Nakuwundi is a member of the Friends church in Burundi and a School Supervisor charged with Peace Education in Bujumbura, Burundi.

Albert Ndlovu is a pastor with the Brethren in Christ Church in Bulawayo, Zimbabwe, and has been a pastor for almost thirty years. He has served on a number of peace and justice committees. They include Grace to Heal; and the Zimbabwe Alliance and Association of Evangelical Christians in Africa—the Ethics, Peace, and Justice desk.

Patson Netha is the executive for the Association of Evangelicals in Africa. Located in Bulawayo, Zimbabwe, his has been a strong voice for healing victims of politically motivated violence.

David Niyonzima is Pastor of Kamenge Friends Church in Burundi and Coordinator of Trauma Healing and Reconciliation Services (THARS).

Cecile Nyiramana works with the Women's Department of the Rwanda Friends Yearly Meeting. She is the founder of the Women in Dialogue Group as a peacemaker who wanted to contribute to the Rwanda Reconciliation Process. She is also Kigali Quarterly Meeting Peace Committee President.

Toma Hamidu Ragnjiya is Peace Co-ordinator for EYN (Church of the Brethren in Nigeria) with a focus on promoting peace and peaceful coexistence in the relationship between Christians and Muslims in Nigeria. He is a former president of EYN and has a degree in Conflict Resolution from Eastern Mennonite University in Harrisonburg, Virginia. Currently he is engaged in a doctoral project at Ashland Theological Seminary in Ohio, where he is working on the creation of a peace model that addresses the Christian/Muslim relations in Nigeria. He and his wife Kwanye have five children—two boys and three girls.

Dr. Ann Riggs holds a Ph. D. from the School of Religious Studies at the Catholic University of America, Washington, D.C., and M.Div. and M.Th. degrees from the Divinity School, Duke University, North Carolina, a Methodist institution. She is coauthor of *Introduction to Ecumenism* (Paulist Press, 1998) and coeditor of the journal *Quaker Theology*. She has worked in the Secretariat for Ecumenical and Interreligious Affairs of the United States Conference of Catholic Bishops, Washington, D.C., and currently serves as Associate General Secretary for Faith and Order of the National Council of Churches of Christ in the U.S.A.

Oliver Kisaka Simiyu is Deputy General Secretary of the National Council of Churches of Kenya. Earlier positions included over two years in secondary school education, and thirteen years in leadership development among students in universities and colleges. He has an M.A. in Biblical and Theological Studies from Nairobi Evangelical Graduate School of Theology, Nairobi. Currently he is working on a proposal for a doctoral dissertation. He is married to Lynette F. Kisaka, and they have two girls.

Abraham Wuta Tizhe for the past twenty-three years has been a pastor for EYN (Church of the Brethren in Nigeria). Since 2003 he has been Vice President of EYN. Under the Mission 21 administrative structure, he serves as African Continental Meeting Coordinator. From 1999 to 2003 he was EYN General Secretary. Rev. Tizhe holds an A.B. in Theology and has attended courses in administration/management, peace and advocacy for church leaders, and HIV/AIDS. Rev. Tizhe is from the Kamwe (Higgi) people and was born in 1956 in the Kuburshosho area of Michika Local Government Council of Adamawa State. He is married to Ladi A. Wuta, and they have four children—a girl and three boys.

Siaka Traore is a Mennonite pastor in Burkina Faso in West Africa and leads the Mennonite church in that country. He is also Chairman of the International Central Council of Africa Inter-Mennonite Mission and is completing a five-year commitment with Mennonite Central Committee as Peace Program Director in West Africa. He came from a Muslim background before becoming a Christian.

Paulus Widjaja is a Mennonite professor, a member of the Faculty of Theology at Duta Wacana Christian University, Jogjakarta, Indonesia.